Christmas Grace
and Other Cycle A Sermons for Advent, Christmas, Epiphany

*Based on the Second Readings
of the Revised Common Lectionary*

Timothy J. Smith

CSS Publishing Co., Inc.
Lima, Ohio

CHRISTMAS GRACE

FIRST EDITION
Copyright © 2010
by CSS Publishing Co., Inc.

Published by CSS Publishing Company, Inc., Lima, Ohio 45807. All rights reserved. No part of this publication may be reproduced in any manner whatsoever without the prior permission of the publisher, except in the case of brief quotations embodied in critical articles and reviews. Inquiries should be addressed to: CSS Publishing Company, Inc., Permissions Department, 5450 N. Dixie Highway, Lima, Ohio 45807.

Scripture quotations marked (NRSV) are from the New Revised Standard Version of the Bible, copyright 1989 by the Division of Christian Education of the Natioanl Counsil of the Churches of Christ in the USA. Used by permission.

Library of Congress Cataloging-in-Publication Data

Smith, Timothy J., 1957-
   Christmas grace and other cycle A sermons for Advent, Christmas, and Epiphany : based on the second readings of the Revised common lectionary / Timothy J. Smith. -- 1st ed.
   p. cm.
   ISBN 0-7880-2628-3 (alk. paper)
   1. Advent sermons. 2. Christmas sermons. 3. Epiphany--Sermons. 4. Common lectionary (1992) I. Title.
  BV4254.5.S65   2010
  252'.612--dc22

2010039621

ISBN-13: 978-0-7880-2628-7
ISBN-10: 0-7880-2628-3

PRINTED IN USA

In Memory of:
James Lee Smith
1933-2008

In Honor of:
wife Donna,
children Becca and new son-in-law Pat
Matt

I thank God for bringing all of you into my life!

Introduction

Our son Matthew was entering the sixth grade when we moved to our new home after too many years of living in parsonages. What I remember most of that first year was how thrilled Matt was to hang Christmas lights outside of our home. He took charge, hanging strings of lights over our garage, and in the trees in front of our house. That night, after dark, he enthusiastically summoned us outside to see his marvelous creation. We stood at the end of the driveway as he turned on the lights. He kept repeating, "Doesn't it look great?" His enthusiasm was contagious that Christmas. The lights also served to remind us that Jesus Christ, the true Light of the world, has come to bring light to all the dark places in our world and in our lives.

I was reminded that December each night as I returned home and saw the simple strings of colored lights that the light continues to shine through the darkest nights of the year. Our modest decorations were no comparison to some of the more elaborate displays in our neighborhood, but we were happy to celebrate our Savior's birth with colorful lights.

While most people claim Advent and Christmas as their favorite time of the year, it frequently presents a challenge for preachers not to rush to Christmas. Each Sunday there are stops we must make on our way to Bethlehem that prepare us spiritually for the birth of our Savior.

Then when life returns to normal early in the New Year, the season of Epiphany is a wonderful opportunity to teach about discipleship. The apostle Paul's letter to the Corinthians allows us to examine our own churches. As we discover some of the errors of the Corinthians we can see ourselves as well. There are times when trivial issues distract or even derail the mission of the church. When that happens Paul gives practical advice for getting back on track.

This collection of sermons on the epistle lessons is offered to stimulate further thought and discussion as we enter the second decade of the twenty-first century.

Timothy J. Smith
May 1, 2009

Table of Contents

Wake Up Call   11
Advent 1
Romans 13:11-14

Unity and Hope   17
Advent 2
Romans 15:4-13

Waiting for Christmas   23
Advent 3
James 5:7-10

The Total Gift   29
Advent 4
Romans 1:1-7

The Best Gift of All   35
Christmas Eve / Day
Titus 2:11-14

The Gift that Matters!   41
Christmas 1
Hebrews 2:10-18

Signed, Sealed, and Delivered   47
Christmas 2
Ephesians 1:3-14

The Light Has Come   53
The Epiphany of Our Lord
Ephesians 3:1-12

Spirit-Direct   59
The Baptism of Our Lord
Epiphany 1
Ordinary Time 1
Acts 10:34-43

The Church is the Place   65
Epiphany 2
Ordinary Time 2
1 Corinthians 1:1-9

Divided We Fall   73
Epiphany 3
Ordinary Time 3
1 Corinthians 1:10-18

Lift High the Cross   79
Epiphany 4
Ordinary Time 4
1 Corinthians 1:18-31

Discerning in Love   85
Epiphany 5
Ordinary Time 5
1 Corinthians 2:1-12 (13-16)

Grow Up!   91
Epiphany 6
Ordinary Time 6
1 Corinthians 3:1-9

Building a Solid Foundation   97
Epiphany 7
Ordinary Time 7
1 Corinthians 3:10-11, 16-23

Praise and Blame 103
Epiphany 8
Ordinary Time 8
1 Corinthians 4:1-5

Everyone Is Invited 109
Epiphany 9
Ordinary Time 9
Romans 1:16-17; 3:22b-28 (29-31)

Credible Witnesses 115
The Transfiguration of Our Lord
(Last Sunday after Epiphany)
2 Peter 1:16-21

Advent 1
Romans 13:11-14

Wake Up Call

Advent always seems out of place with everything else that is going on around us. While people are rushing toward Christmas in a shopping frenzy our observance is markedly different. Sometimes we get so lost in the sentiment and traditions of Christmas that we have difficulty connecting with the themes of Advent. Advent is about waiting expectantly while longing for God to act. However, we must admit that we grow impatient and demand immediate satisfaction.

The first Sunday of Advent finds us not dreaming of the perfect Christmas or searching for a gift for the person who has everything, but rather looking to the future — to the second coming of Christ. Advent begins not with a baby in a manger but rather, looking forward to the return of our Lord and Savior Jesus Christ.

The apostle Paul along with first-century Christians believed that Jesus would return during their own lifetime. While they were waiting they believed that Jesus would return any day. Much of Paul's writings reveal the notion that Jesus would return within a short period of time. Expecting Christ's return any day would certainly alter the way you live your life and what you view as important.

We do not have that same sense of urgency today as Paul and the early believers. Nearly 2,000 years have passed and we are still waiting for Christ's triumphant return. Advent reminds us that our faith is future oriented, propelling us to the future. Too often our focus is on the past, which makes it difficult to ponder what tomorrow will bring. While it may not always seem to be the case, we believe that with Jesus the best is always yet to come.

On this first Sunday of Advent the apostle Paul encourages us to "know what time it is." It is time for us to focus on Jesus, refraining from all other distractions commonly associated with Christmas. "Now is the moment for you to wake from sleep," he writes to believers who might have been going through the motions without realizing the importance of the day.

The people had better wake up and pay attention, "for salvation is nearer to us now than when we first became believers," Paul writes. We've been here before, working our way toward Christmas. It is easy to simply go through the motions, expecting nothing out of the ordinary to happen.

Paul commands us to wake up, pay attention; "the night is far gone," God is at work in our lives and in our world. We will not want to miss anything due to our inattention.

As we focus or refocus on Jesus we reject the "works of darkness." There is evil in our world, causing us at times to stumble and fall, yet Paul instructs believers to live in the light of Christ. The light of Christ dispels the darkness. Paul uses the metaphor of suiting up with the "armor of light." The armor of light will provide protection as we confront the evil powers and injustices of this world. We dress in the armor of light to shine brightly through the darkness of evil. We do so knowing that ultimately Christ will prevail over the darkness of evil.

We strive to follow the positive command to "put on the Lord Jesus Christ" rejecting works of the flesh that hamper our relationship with Jesus. Our enemies are "not flesh and blood" but rather the destructive power that enslave and divide people — mistrust, injustice, addictions, thirst for revenge, prejudice, fear, and greed.

Late on Christmas Day the Lawder family of Atlanta gathers around the Christmas tree. There is one more gift to open, and it's the one they anticipate the most every year, a plain white envelope. Their daughter-in-law reads the note inside the envelope that states that their parents have supported a local health clinic in the children's honor. Everyone smiles, some with tears streaming down their faces. "It's the best part of the holiday," one of the sons claims.

"Our parents raised us to believe that giving back is important," says another son. "We worked at soup kitchens and we always had people over for Christmas dinner who had nowhere else to go." The children now in their twenties continue the tradition by supporting Heifer International, which provides milk for a third-world village; helped refurbish a Katrina victim's house; and bought ornaments for the church, all in honor of their parents. Of this yearly tradition their mother says, "My sons love seeing how they can make me cry each year." She remembers how one year her sons helped a single mother and her children. "They wanted this family to have the kind of day we have," she says. "When she called to thank them I cried."[1]

During Advent our focus is on living as the light of Christ, diligently working to help other people. We need to remember whose birthday we are preparing to celebrate — not our own but Jesus'. Jesus certainly had a passion for helping other people. We strive to be like Jesus in all we say and do.

"Put on the Lord Jesus Christ" reminds us of our baptisms and our profession of faith. Elsewhere Paul states, "As many of you as were baptized into Christ have clothed yourselves with Christ" (Galatians 3:27). We "put on" so that everything we do, we do as committed disciples of Jesus Christ. Everything we say, we do so as an agent of Jesus. Living out our baptism in this manner often will lead to conflict with the status quo, but we are clothed in the armor of light for protection.

Wake up, pay attention, and put on the "armor of Light" that will transform and change all aspects of our lives, including how we prepare to celebrate Christ's birth in our lives. Advent is about turning to something far better than what is left behind.

The first Sunday of Advent is about waking up from our slumber to pay attention to God's Word for us as we prepare to receive God's gift once again. We wait for that glorious day when Jesus shall return. Meanwhile we continue doing those things that Jesus would want us to do, loving and caring for others, confronting evil in our communities and world.

"I do not have the time for this," muttered Kregg Grippo. Kregg owns a small contracting company in upstate New York. A friend of a friend asked if he could help an elderly woman who lost her home to fire. However, Kregg had second thoughts when he saw the extensive damage to the modest house. "What am I supposed to do," he thought to himself, "build her a new house?" He did not have the time to build a new house with Christmas only a couple of weeks away.

When he met the elderly woman he discovered that she went to school with his aunt. She told him about the fire and how she could not extinguish it. By the time the fire department arrived it was too late. She told him that she had lived there for sixty years. Kregg asked her where she was staying and she led him to a shed in her backyard. She was sleeping on an old cot covered with afghans. "She should not be staying here," he thought.

Even though he did not have time he assured her not to worry because he would take care of everything. "You'll have a new house by Christmas" he promised.

Kregg called everyone he knew, his crew, suppliers, even a competitor or two asking for their help. He asked customers to give him an extension on other projects. Within days fifteen people arrived ready to work. They would donate their time, "Somehow," Kregg thought, "we're going to make this happen." Word spread, the next morning twenty people showed up, then thirty, then a local TV station. The story ran on the evening news. As a result an electrical contractor called offering to help, as did a roofing company, as well as heating supply companies, and carpet suppliers. It seemed everyone wanted to help this woman.

They finished the house on Christmas Eve. The ranch house had new appliances and was furnished with new furniture as well. Some of the workers even bought the woman Christmas presents. "It was the smallest home I'd ever built," Kregg says, "but it gave me the biggest feeling I'd ever had."[2]

The apostle Paul asks us if we know what time it is. Our response is that today and every day is God's time — it is the time for us to get our act together, living in the light, transcending the darkness all around us to celebrate a Savior who can and does change lives. Amen.

---

1. Sally Stich, "The Best Gift of All," *Woman's Day*, December 4, 2007, pp. 54-57.
2. Kregg Grippo, "Last-Minute Miracle," *Guideposts*, December 2005, pp. 36-38.

Advent 2
Romans 15:4-13

Unity and Hope

As we make our way through Advent inching closer to Christmas, our days are consumed with many tasks. Our "to do" list grows each day. At times we are often out of breath and wondering if we will complete everything on our list before Christmas Day. We gather on this Second Sunday in Advent to spiritually prepare for what God has done and continues to do in our lives and in our world. We have been too busy with all our activities and tasks so that we are in danger of missing out on the miracle of Christmas. We come in the language of John the Baptist to "Prepare the way" removing all the clutter from our lives to experience once again the birth of our Savior.

"For me," Patty Kirk writes, "the waiting is complicated by anxiety and doubt. Will joy ever come?" At some point she claims that joy does come. "Sometimes a song at church cheers me, or an act of kindness from one of my daughters. Once, it was the hilarious moment when, while decorating our tree, we discovered my previous year's present from my mother-in-law."[1]

Instead of feeling overwhelmed by empty tasks we can turn to the Bible. The stories of faith contained within scripture actually become our own story. The examples of faith are meant to encourage us in our faith walk. At those times when nothing seems to be going the way we desire, we turn to the stories of faith and are encouraged through the example of those who have gone before us.

The apostle Paul, writing to the church at Rome, a church he had not yet visited, made an amazing claim, "For whatever was written in former days was written for our instruction, so that by steadfastness and by the encouragement of the scriptures we might have hope." When we discover how others dealt with a variety of problems and setbacks yet held on to their faith, we know that we too will make it through the rough times. By reflecting on biblical characters we are encouraged to continue on our journey of faith filled with hope.

We find that those who cling to faith are able to endure much adversity in their lives. When we read such examples we are filled with a fresh sense of hope, those heroes of faith made it through difficult days so we too will endure.

As we read our Bibles daily this sense of hope is instilled within us. We think of people we know who do not have this sense of hopefulness but are mired in a pit of despair. The focus of Advent is that God has already acted in sending Jesus to us while the message of Christmas is that God loves and cares for all people. According to the apostle Paul one of the reasons Jesus came to live among us was to break down all the barriers that divided people. Throughout Jesus' earthly ministry he repeatedly broke down cultural and social barriers. Jesus shocked the religious leaders by eating and socializing with prostitutes, tax collectors, and other sinners. "This fellow welcomes sinners and eats with them" (Luke 15:2) the religious leaders complained not understanding why Jesus would want to spend time with people they believed to be undesirable. Jesus showed love and respect to all people. He broke down the barriers that existed between women and men, Jews and Samaritans.

Paul repeatedly addressed tensions in the life of the early church. The first believers were from a Jewish background. Although they claimed Jesus as their Lord and Savior they continued to keep the laws of the Torah. Problems arose when people came to know Jesus who did not come from that same background. Would they have to observe Jewish practices before becoming believers? Paul championed the cause of Gentiles (those who were not Jewish), breaking down the barriers that separated and divided people. Paul pleaded his case of unity in the name of Christ to those who at first were reluctant. Paul wrote, "To live in harmony with one another, in accordance with Christ Jesus."

Instead of seeing only the obvious differences, Paul urged the believers to celebrate their unity in Christ. Elsewhere Paul claims, "There is no longer Jew or Greek, there is no longer slave or free, there is no longer male and female; for all of you are one in Christ Jesus" (Galatians 3:28). These were radical words in a time when people were defined by their heritage, gender, and social class. When you stop to think about it, those words continue to be revolutionary today. We are to love and accept people who have different life experiences than we do; we can make them feel welcome at our church.

Paul always was the pragmatist and quoted scripture to drive home his point. "Therefore I will confess you among the Gentiles, and sing praises to your name," and "Praise the Lord, all you Gentiles, and let all the peoples praise him." Without question Paul believed that in Christ all earthly differences were no longer important for all were one in Christ.

A Vietnam veteran recalls an experience he had on Christmas Eve in 1972. His squad was ambushed by the enemy, everyone was killed except him. Following a struggle and with great force he was captured. "I was thinking how much I did not want to spend Christmas, let alone the remaining six months of my tour of duty, in a POW camp," he explains.

They kept traveling through the night. When they finally stopped the Vietnamese lieutenant gave him food to eat. "Merry Christmas" he said in perfect English. His captor told him it would be an honor to celebrate Christmas with him. His name was Nugent. He explained that he had been educated in Canada and that his family had been killed. "Silent Night" was Nugent's favorite Christmas Carol. The two men began singing it together.

Early the next morning shots rang out. "Bullets were flying all around," the American soldier recalls. Nugent was shot in the chest. He held him in his arms. "Thanking me for the Christmas songfest." He started singing "Silent Night" knowing that it was Nugent's favorite carol.

"Nugent put his bloody hand to my lips, 'the voice of angel, I go in peace.' Thank you were his last words. At that moment I did not see an enemy, but a friend and a brother. Here was a man who started as an enemy, showed compassion, became a friend, died as a brother."[2] God loves and cares for all people and we should do the same.

The message of Advent is to continue to break down the barriers that divide people today. As modern-day disciples of Jesus we strive for harmony and unity. We sing, "Let There Be Peace on Earth" the last line states "and let it begin with me."[3] What better time of the year to seek reconciliation with those we might not have seen eye to eye with during the year. When we are able to do this we are one step closer to peace on earth. "Welcome one another, therefore, just as Christ has welcomed you, for the glory of God," Paul penned. Paul knew the importance of welcoming and accepting others into the fellowship. May each one of us make an extra effort to welcome people to our church this month.

As Paul read the scriptures and prayed he concluded that Jesus came to this earth for all people. That all people be united in Christ was God's ultimate plan for humanity. As we live out our faith in our church, in our community, and ultimately in our world, we do so knowing that we are part of God's larger plan. Like the prophets of old, we might not live to see the results of all of our efforts, but we continue in the name of Christ, trusting that God will bless our efforts.

It was as if Paul visualized Jesus surrounded by all people, Jew and Gentile alike when he wrote, "So that together you may with one voice glorify the God and Father of our Lord Jesus Christ."

The stories of faith inspire and encourage us in our daily lives. We reach out to others breaking down the barriers that divide people knowing that we are part of God's divine drama. Our closing verse serves as Paul's desire, "May the God of hope fill you with all joy and peace in believing, so that you may abound in hope by the power of the Holy Spirit." As we live out our faith fresh hope is instilled in us which yields to joy. Amen.

---

1. Patty Kirk, "Slower than Christmas" *Today's Christian Woman*, December 23, 2008.
2. Delilah, *Love Matters* (Ontario Canada: Harlequin, 2008), pp. 43-47.
3. "Let There Be Peace on Earth," The United Methodist Hymnal, 1989, #431.

Advent 3
James 5:7-10

Waiting for Christmas

Excitement is building on this the third Sunday of Advent knowing that Christmas will soon be here. Children have made their Christmas wish lists of all the wonderful things they desire. Some might have had long lists while others might have subtracted an item or two, still others might have added a few more gifts during the past weeks. We have heard people ask, "What do you want for Christmas?" Most of us, young and old alike, have no problem sharing our wish list with anyone who asks.

On our mad rush to Christmas we pause and ask ourselves two very important questions: What do you really want? And what will make a difference in your life this Christmas? Our goal come Christmas Day is to be different as a result of our spiritual preparation during our Advent journey.

The book of James is filled with much practical advice for those striving to live the Christian life. The apostle James believed that genuine faith results in outward actions and responses. The way we treat each other speaks volumes about our own understanding of faith. If we do nothing to help a sister or brother who is going through a difficult time, then we need to seriously re-examine our faith. James bluntly declares, "So faith by itself, if it has no works, is dead."

There might very well have been some tension in the early church between believers, which resulted in some grumbling. Some might have grown impatient waiting for the Lord Jesus to return. It is in this context that James exhorts believers to, "be patient." As we have discovered people living in the first century literally believed that Jesus would return any day; most certainly within their lifetime.

A crisis of faith occurred when Jesus did not immediately return. That was the situation James addressed in his letter.

Many of us struggle with being patient. We want what we want when we want it and do not like to wait. Elementary school teachers will tell us that the week before Christmas break the children are overly excited and can barely concentrate on their lessons as they day dream of opening their presents on Christmas Day. We want to hurry up and get to Christmas and skip the preliminaries. Our impatience tempts us to take short cuts that ultimately dilute the experience.

One person describes, "We yanked the tree out of the box and then plugged it right into the wall." Another said, "The tree was pre-decorated with colored lights and a bunch of ornaments. It took three minutes tops — none of this three hours and listen to Christmas music nonsense for me!"

Instead of thoughtfully searching for special gifts for loved ones someone bragged how he avoided the crowded mall. "Fifteen gift cards from the same web site," he boasted. "Three clicks of the mouse and a credit card number. In and out: five minutes and I'm done."

Derek Maul understands the value of decorating with his family. He writes, "Each ornament on our tree represents something unique. The bumble bee angel the children made, the stained-glass bell lovingly crafted by an old friend. The treasured cornhusk seraph we found in Appalachia the week we discovered we were expecting our first child, the doll Rebekah brought back from Haiti that gently reminds us Christ came for everyone."[1]

It takes time and patience to reach worthwhile goals in life. Students know they have to finish school before embarking on a career. It takes years and a lot of hard work to reach their goals. The person starting a new job knows it takes time to fully understand their tasks and responsibilities. There are certain things in life that cannot be "fast-forwarded" to get to the good part.

Farmers know what it is to wait patiently. They cultivate their fields, plant seeds, and wait for rain and sun to nurture their crops. An entire harvest can be either helped or hindered by weather conditions. Not enough rain and there is no crop to harvest. Too much rain can ruin and destroy what was planted. The farmer plants and then trusts that God will provide.

James lifts up farmers as an example of people who have learned to wait. Another example is "the prophets who spoke in the name of the Lord." Prophets speak the Word of God but seldom see immediate results. Not only do they not see the fruit of their ministry but often suffer as a result of proclaiming what God has placed on their hearts. Patience yields to trust.

In the same way we place our trust in God. We do not know what the future holds for us; yet we place our trust in God.

While we patiently wait we follow James' advice to "strengthen your hearts." We strengthen our hearts by keeping our focus and concentrating on what really matters in our life — our relationship with Jesus Christ. It is easy, especially this time of year, to get sidetracked and lose our way. Remember being busy is not a substitute for being faithful. We keep our focus this season on God's most precious gift — Jesus Christ. We need to let go of everything else and concentrate on what really matters.

Waiting patiently does not mean that we just do nothing. We do not passively sit in our easy chairs and wait but instead continue to participate in what Jesus calls us and expects us to do. Ours is an active waiting.

The year had been a difficult one for Rae Smith who lost her job for the second time in two years. Without a severance package to keep her afloat, time was her enemy. "I was feeling really down," she says.

The one Saturday near the end of November her mother called with more bad news. The annual community Christmas program had fallen on hard times. Donations of food and gifts for the children were down. Many members of the community choir, the program sponsor, were unable to contribute as they had in the past. Rae had witnessed the cheer the program brought to children in need. As she talked with her mother she resolved to continue with the annual Christmas program.

Rae called every local merchant she could think of and explained the problem seeking their financial support. She wrote letters to friends and neighbors asking for donations. Within 24 hours she had collected 500 toys and gifts from area merchants. She was overwhelmed — overjoyed at the outpouring from the community. The Christmas program turned out to be a great success!

This is not the end of the story, one month later Rae landed a well-paying job. She reflects on the December that changed her life. The moment she reached out to help others, she says, God reached down and helped her.[2]

With a careful reading of the Bible we discover that God is very patient with humanity. We learn that patience is a characteristic of God. We need to exhibit that same sense of patience with each other, as well as, when we share our faith with those outside of our church.

We must live out our faith as if our Lord Jesus Christ is standing at our door ready to enter. James writes, "The Judge is standing at the doors!" Our behavior would be quite different if we knew that Jesus is standing at our door. Elsewhere in the New Testament we see Jesus poised to enter, "I am standing at the door, knocking; if you hear my voice and open the door, I will come in to you and eat with you, and you with me" (Revelation 3:20). There are famous paintings showing Jesus standing at the door. In our busyness will we be able to hear Jesus knocking on our door?

When we become impatient and lose our center we sometimes turn against one another. Our disagreements with our family or church members can escalate into harsh words spoken resulting in strained and broken relationships. There are times when we allow our differences to become mountains instead of remaining molehills. Passionately James writes, "Beloved, do not grumble against one another, so that you may not be judged."

Perhaps the real test of faith is endurance. Can we continue to live out our faith without becoming discouraged and turning against one another? We wait. We endure some difficult times knowing that the rough times are not God's final answer for us. We will make it through. God will see us through!

"Christmas was always my favorite time of the year," Noel states. She particularly enjoyed the family get-togethers and the caroling. However her celebration of Christmas has changed over the years. Over a short period of time both her parents died, she lost contact with her three siblings, and her only son moved across the country. "Christmas get-togethers ceased," she explains, "caroling was just another part of a church service." Christmas became a lonely season for her.

"My discomfort forced me to realize that I had allowed my family's traditions to take the focus away from Christ," she writes. "Once I put Christ back in the center, Christmas again became my favorite time of the year — not because of outworn pleasures but because of God's gift on the first Christmas." Noel realized that she is part of a much larger family — "God's family."[3]

We've made our lists and checked them twice. We know exactly what we want. However, only Jesus knows what we really need. There is a difference between what we want and what we really need. Only Jesus knows the difference. Jesus will soon be here; will we be ready? Come Lord Jesus into our hearts. Amen.

---

1. Derek Maul, *In My Heart I Carry A Star* (Nashville: Upper Room Books, 2008), p. 57.
2. Gracie Bonds, "Sharing the Miracles in our Lives," *Atlanta-Journal Constitution*, Staples-staff, December 21, 2002.
3. Noel S. McArtor, "God's Family," *Upper Room*, December 18, 2008.

Advent 4
Romans 1:1-7

The Total Gift

It is easy to get so caught up in the sentimentality and nostalgia of Christmas that we neglect the true reason we celebrate. We receive Christmas cards portraying a cute infant Jesus lying in a manger filled with straw. The Baby Jesus is pictured in the center with Mary and Joseph on one side, the shepherds and Magi on the other. We know this scene: animals are in the background, in the distance angels can be seen hovering, as a star shines brightly overhead. However, there is more to Advent and Christmas than celebrating the birth of a baby. Babies make no demands on anyone other than their parents or those caring for them. While we may enjoy holding babies, the moment they start fussing we quickly hand them back to their mother or father.

If we forever view Jesus as an infant we miss out on much of his life and teachings. The Lord Jesus stands before us calling us to follow him. Jesus demands we become intentional in our interactions with other people. We are to pay attention to people often forgotten or overlooked in our communities and world, just as Jesus did. If we volunteer at homeless shelters or donate money to support local charities, we show that we care about all people just as Jesus taught us. It's easier to simply view Jesus as a cute little baby who makes no demands on our lives.

Karen recalls the year her parents retired and moved to Florida. Her parents decided to stop exchanging Christmas gifts and instead give donations to charities, "using the money they would have spent on each other," she explains her parents gave, "dog food for the Humane Society, canned goods to a homeless shelter, toys to Toys for Tots."

The family welcomed this new gift strategy. Karen says her mother would buy dolls on sale throughout the year. "Then a few weeks before Christmas she'd assemble kits with a doll, at least five new outfits, accessories… and donate them to a worthy organization." Karen and her family joined the project.

Even though Karen's mother died a few years ago, her project lives on "as our family stockpiles dolls and outfits for next Christmas. I smile," Karen reflects, "remembering Mom's delight in her dolls and her pleasure in giving joy to others."[1]

The apostle Paul knew firsthand the demands Jesus makes on all who follow him. Paul was writing to the church at Rome, a church he had not yet visited. In the opening verses, wanting to make a good impression, Paul identifies himself as "a servant of Jesus Christ." Paul was clear about his position: a servant serves the master. He was a humble servant of the Lord Jesus. He was "called to be an apostle," through his conversion experience on the Damascus Road where he met the Lord Jesus. It was then that he was, "set apart for the gospel of God." From that moment on Paul would spend the rest of his life laboring for the Lord Jesus. More than that, Paul was willing to give up his entire life, everything he had labored for up to that moment, to put himself to use for Jesus. Because of that powerful experience Paul completely surrendered to his Lord. We are called to follow Jesus just as Paul was called.

Paul in his opening words to the Romans makes the case that Jesus was the long-awaited messiah. The Old Testament prophets foretold of the coming of God's messiah hundreds of years before the birth of Jesus. Isaiah told of God giving a sign for all the people, "Look, the young woman is with child and shall bear a son, and shall name him Immanuel" (Isaiah 7:14). For centuries the people held certain expectations of what the messiah would be like and what he would accomplish. In truth, Jesus did not exactly fit many of these preconceived notions, but was nonetheless the long-awaited messiah.

Jesus was a descendant of King David, Paul states, "according to the flesh." People were looking for a messiah from the royal house of David. Joseph was a direct descendant of David. In this morning's gospel reading (Matthew 1:18-25), Joseph is charged with the responsibility of naming the baby Jesus. Joseph would raise Jesus as any parent would. Jesus was no ordinary baby. Jesus was God in the flesh. That is what incarnation means — God became one of us in Jesus!

During his life Jesus experienced everything that we do, the full range of emotions from grief and despair, to joy and triumph. We are able to closely identify with Jesus knowing that through his life he experienced the same ups and downs that we do. Jesus knows just what we are going through. Jesus is the "Son of God" both divine and human.

While some might have had questions whether or not Jesus was the messiah, Paul states that all doubts were erased by the resurrection. Jesus was "declared to be Son of God with power according to the spirit of holiness by resurrection from the dead." Here we are just days from Christmas and we are reminded of Easter and the resurrection. These two events should not and cannot be separated. The incarnation, the birth of Jesus, and how God raised him to new life define the essence of our faith.

It is through God's amazing grace that we are included among the children of God. It is through Jesus that "we have received grace." God's grace is freely given and is not something that we ever earn or even deserve. Elsewhere Paul makes the astonishing claim that we are saved through grace. "For by grace you have been saved through faith, and this is not your own doing; it is the gift of God" (Ephesians 2:8).

Paul was writing with the hope of convincing the people of the reality of the gospel message that he experienced at his conversion. Without question, Jesus is the long-awaited messiah foretold by the prophets. Jesus taught, healed the sick, and won followers. Evil put Jesus to death but God raised him to new life on Easter. This is the foundation of our faith and is cause for celebration. Paul was convinced beyond a shadow of doubt that all this was true. And Paul wanted his readers, and all of us, to believe the same about Jesus Christ.

There were problems within the early church that Paul patiently addressed time and time again. One problem that continued to surface was accepting people who were not of Jewish descent. Much of Paul's writings covered this subject. God's grace includes all people, "including yourselves who are called to belong to Jesus Christ." The ethnic makeup of the Roman church included Gentiles, but because of their faith in Jesus Christ, Paul labels them as "saints." "To all God's beloved in Rome, who are called to be saints," the apostle wrote. They were saints, loved by God.

Cimeri was traveling home for Christmas, from California to Arkansas by bus, taking her two young sons to see their grandfather. Life was difficult; she was broke. The reason she was headed home was that her father had wired her enough money for bus fare and food for the four-day journey. Cimeri was afraid to tell him how bad things were and that she wanted to move back home with him for a few months until she could get back on her feet.

Two hours from Kansas City, at four o'clock in the morning, the bus lurched to a stop jolting everyone awake. The bus had broken down. By the time they got to the station they had already missed the connecting bus for Arkansas. The next bus would leave in twelve hours. Cimeri called her father in tears, "We're not going to make it in time for Christmas Eve," she said. Checking her purse she had only ten dollars — not enough for a real meal. What was she going to do?

A tall man dressed in overalls and a Santa cap was walking around the bus station handing out things to people. "Look kids," she exclaimed, "it's Santa Claus." The man stopped in front of them. "Merry Christmas" he said as he reached into his pocket and pulled out a hundred dollar bill. "I can't accept this," Cimeri gasped, waving his hand away. "Are these your boys?" he asked. He reached into his pocket and pulled out two more $100 bills.

With tears in her eyes she told the stranger how badly she needed the money but there was no way she could accept it. The man bent down and told her he knew exactly what it felt like to be down on your luck. He reached into his pocket once more and pulled out an additional two hundred dollars. "Take it" he said gently. She broke down and told him how they had no money, how the bus broken down, and that they would not reach their destination for Christmas Eve. The man promised that she would be home that night; he arranged a limousine to take her and her sons home. This was a moment of grace and through this stranger's kindness she did make it home for Christmas. And in the process her faith in Jesus Christ was restored.[2]

Christmas Day will soon be here. We have been preparing for that day through these four weeks of Advent. We have spent these days preparing our hearts and minds to receive Jesus Christ, God's gift to us. These weeks of Advent we have been changed and transformed as we reflect on our faith in light of the scriptures we have examined. It is with humble obedience that we approach the manger. From that cute little baby who grew up to be our Lord we can experience life in its fullness. It is from that manger that we are called to a lifetime of discipleship. We follow Jesus, doing what he would want us to do. When we do that we experience the grace and peace that come from "God our Father and the Lord Jesus Christ."

On Christmas Day we will be spiritually ready to receive Jesus once again into our lives. We will be prepared to enter into the joy of the coming year, ready to claim the grace that comes to us in Jesus. Amen.

---

1. Karen M. Leet, "Christmas in June," *Guideposts*, June 2008, p. 19.
2. Cimeri Miller, "Along Came Santa," *Guideposts*, December 2007, pp. 22-24.

Christmas Eve / Day
Titus 2:11-14

The Best Gift of All

There is a special feeling from being in church on Christmas Eve. For many of us it feels like coming home for Christmas. We come to hear the familiar story of Mary and Joseph making their way to the little town of Bethlehem. We hear once again of Baby Jesus born in stable. Soon after an unexpected encounter with angels, the shepherds head to the manger to see Jesus for themselves. Children have creatively acted out this story for generations complete with the wise men offering their gifts. Living Nativities complete with live animals are portrayed in church parking lots in many communities. The story of Jesus' birth has become part of who we are; it is our story. There is something very familiar as well as comforting about being in church tonight.

Unfortunately some people never move beyond viewing Jesus as a cute infant lying on a bed of straw. They see nothing more than a little baby wrapped in "swaddling" cloths, lying in a manger. To truly celebrate Christmas we need the rest of the story, to view Jesus not only as an infant but also as our Lord and Savior who calls us to follow him. For our lives to truly be changed by the birth of Jesus requires that we examine his entire life and teachings, so that we can see the whole picture.

The apostle Paul was writing to one of his traveling companions, Titus, to encourage his friend and the other believers on the tiny island of Crete. There was controversy as the believers struggled with questions of law and how to deal with others whose view of faith was quite different from their own. Paul heard of their present difficulties and wanted them to remain focused on Jesus. It is so easy for us to become distracted with so many other matters. There are times when we need to be reminded of who we are and what we believe; that is one of the reasons we are gathered here tonight.

"For the grace of God has appeared," Paul wrote, "bringing salvation to all." According to Paul's understanding it was God's intent from the very beginning to bring salvation to all people. Christmas serves to remind us that Jesus came for all people. The angel told the shepherds, "I am bringing you good news of great joy for all the people." "Great joy for all people" was God's goal from the moment of creation. The early church struggled over cultural and ethnic differences; however, Paul and others believed that the good news is that Jesus came for all people. That is why people with different life experiences are always welcome in church.

Further we are able to "renounce impiety and worldly passions" knowing that we are to "live lives that are self-controlled, upright, and godly." Elsewhere Paul teaches, "Do not be conformed to this world, but be transformed by the renewing of your minds, so that you may discern what is the will of God — what is good and acceptable and perfect" (Romans 12:2). It is easy to fall into the trap of "worldly passions," and forget that Jesus calls us to "live lives that are self-controlled, upright, and godly." We do not follow the ways of the world as much as we live our lives for Jesus. We must remain focused on Jesus.

We respond to God's grace by responding to Jesus allowing him to enter and change our lives. Our goal is to be more and more like Jesus each and every day in all of our conversations and actions. With Jesus in our lives we cannot help but be changed and transformed, here and now, "in the present age." We are transformed people when we serve others in the name of Jesus.

Rose recalls the Christmas when she was thirteen years old, her father was ill and in the hospital and would not be able to spend Christmas with them. Because of the circumstance, she says, "Christmas for our family was very different from those in the past."

She does not remember if they even had a Christmas tree that year or if there were many gifts. What she does remember is spending Christmas Day at the hospital. It was difficult to see her father in the hospital. When the family had finished their visit she remembers walking through the lobby where there was a large Christmas tree. In that setting the tree seemed stark. Yet, she remembers thinking as they walked out the door, "This is the best Christmas I ever had." She was mystified by that thought. It had been a sparse Christmas and a season filled with anxiety concerning her father's health. But on another level she realized that what made Christmas special was being with people you love. Even though her family was in a trying situation, they had spent the day together.

It would take months for her father to fully recover; during that time her mother had to work. Her meager salary did not cover the family's needs, so the church gave food for Christmas and Thanksgiving as well as other things to help.

Many years have passed; Rose is married and has her own children. She longed to try something different at Christmas. She suggested that instead of buying expensive gifts that they help meet someone else's needs. At first her husband was not too keen on the idea. She made the same suggestion the next year and the next. When her children were older she made the same suggestion but they were not interested either.

One day she explained her desire to make Christmas less commercial and more a time for family to give of themselves to people and families in need. It was a moment of clarity for Rose; she realized that her family did not have the experience she had as a teen, a father ill in the hospital over Christmas. It was then Rose says that she discovered the really important thing about Christmas is people, "and that reaching out to them in love and caring warms the heart and nourishes the spirit. When that happens," she claims, "Christmas is the best it can be."[1] In striving to be like Jesus we see human need through his eyes and we respond as Jesus would.

We come tonight to once again receive the gift God has given us — Jesus Christ. To accept God's gift means welcoming Jesus into our lives. The adult Jesus calls us to follow him and makes demands upon us to reorder our priorities as well as change the direction of our lives.

We still acknowledge the future dimension as well. Paul claims that "while we wait for the blessed hope and the manifestation of the glory of our great God and Savior, Jesus Christ," we are transformed here and now. We wait as people of faith for that future glory. As people of faith we live our lives believing that the best is yet to come.

As we are about to celebrate Christmas we must remember the rest of the story, how Jesus suffered and died on our behalf and how God raised him to new life. That sense of the future is found in the closing verse, "He it is who gave himself for us that he might redeem us from all iniquity and purify for himself a people of his own who are zealous for good deeds." This is the basis of our hope. All we need to do is welcome God's grace into our lives. Grace is a gift to us, not something that we earn, but a true gift given freely.

A gift is a gift because it is given without guarantee of an appropriate response on our parts. What God has done in Jesus is a free gift that inspires an appropriate response in us. God has acted in sending Jesus to us, "bringing salvation for all." On Christmas morning we will open gifts that will bring us temporary joy; however, when we claim Jesus as God's gift to us we experience a profound and lasting sense of joy.

When Derek was attending college he claims that he experienced a crisis in faith. Three days before Christmas he explains, "I suffered a near panic attack when it dawned on me that I had yet to experience even a morsel of a twinge of genuine seasonal peace." In a rush of homesickness, he blamed the palm trees and the green grass and Florida's warm nights for the way he was feeling. He was convinced that the only possible road to receive Advent peace required a trip down memory lane into Christmas past.

He arranged a last minute flight home to London. His parents met him at the airport and welcomed him home. That day he walked to the town center like he used to, remembering the festive decorations and atmosphere of his youth. "I wanted to jump up and down stomping my feet and clapping my hands," he says.

It had been a long night of travel, he had not slept a wink, and admits to being "breathless with excitement because I couldn't allow myself to understand that I felt so empty inside because I had forgotten about Jesus, the only authentic source of hope, peace, love, and joy I could really ever know." Traveling thousands of miles as well as the familiar surroundings and the comfortable feeling of his hometown were unable to give him the seasonal peace he was looking for. Nothing seemed to be working for Derek.

Not ready to give up, still feeling empty, Derek found a church that offered a late candlelight service. "Sometimes it takes a moment or more of desperation to achieve the kind of clarity necessary to hear God's voice," Derek reflects. Christmas finally hit him as the congregation sang a carol. At that moment he explains, "I felt relieved and forgiven and free." It was then that he received what he was looking for, receiving the peace of Christ. Christmas is about peace and God's grace.[2]

Christmas Eve is a time to receive the gift that God has for each one of us. Just as Jesus was born on this night long ago, so may he be reborn in our hearts and lives. To receive God's gift in our lives anew we must make room for this most precious gift. We come to the manger to embrace the story of Christmas, not as a once a year tradition but as a call upon our lives.

Christmas Eve is a time to recommit our lives to Jesus Christ. We respond to God's Christmas gift for all people by reordering our lives engaging in what Jesus would want us to do, and paying attention to the down and out just as Jesus would. God's gift of Jesus brings out the very best we have to offer. Tonight is the night to receive the gift! Amen.

---

1. Rose Zuzworsky, "The Best Christmas Ever" *Christmas Remembered Ron DelBene*, (Nashville: Upper Room Books, 1991), pp. 35-36.
2. Derek Maul, *In My Heart I Carry A Star* (Nashville: Upper Room Books, 2008), pp. 52-55.

Christmas 1
Hebrews 2:10-18

The Gift that Matters!

As we gather on the Sunday after Christmas we do so with a sigh of relief. The gifts have been opened; our family has come and returned home. The past month typically holds the busiest days and weeks of the year for many of us. It is little wonder why we might feel tired today. It has been a hectic couple of weeks but slowly our lives are returning back to normal, as we settle back into our regular routines.

We have celebrated Jesus' birth. We are reminded that Jesus came to bring salvation to all people. Jesus is God's present to each one of us. We must respond to that gift as well by allowing Jesus to enter and change our lives.

Our focus for the days following Christmas and before the start of the New Year is to reflect on the events of the past year. News magazines have special year end reports highlighting the good and the bad from the previous twelve months. Television news programs will also review what has taken place this year by asking and answering the question of whether or not this has been a good year.

In the same way we reflect on our faith. Has the past year been one of growth or stagnation in our walk with Jesus? For the last month we have focused on the Baby Jesus. We've sung the Christmas carol asking the question, "What Child is This?" We've answered that the baby was none other than our Lord Jesus Christ. Our question this morning is what do we do with Jesus now that we've celebrated Christmas? Do we pack him away with our nativity set only to bring him out next December? Or do we claim or reclaim Jesus as our Lord? A question worthy of our reflection today is how has God's gift — Jesus changed our lives?

Columnist Maureen Dowd recalls the Christmas that she received "one of those wooden horses that bounced on springs." She named her horse "Trigger" and rode him every day.

Much to her dismay one morning she discovered that her beloved horse was gone. Her mother explained that a poor woman and her son spotted Trigger as they walked past their house. The young boy "stared longingly at the horse." Maureen recalls how her mother's world had been turned upside down when she lost her own father at age twelve. As a result her mother always had a soft spot for children who were hurt and in need. On a modest pension her mother would send a few dollars to children who she had read about who were hungry or in need of an operation.

Maureen did not want to accept the news that her horse was given to another child, a stranger. "I was crushed," she writes. Whenever she and her mother disagreed over the next sixteen years Maureen would always bring up her beloved horse that her mother had given away.

Then on her 21st birthday, Maureen came home to find her bouncing horse with a handwritten note in its mouth, "I'm back!" signed "Trigger." Many years have passed and Maureen is thankful for the lesson her mother taught her at a young age, "materialism and narcissism can only smother life — and Christmas — if you let them."[1]

The author of the book of Hebrews gives us a different perspective on Jesus' life. Hebrews was addressed to people who had gone through a tough time, a time of suffering, persecution, imprisonment, and confiscation of property. The author wrote hoping to instill a fresh sense of hope, desiring people to turn to Jesus.

We discover that the author claims that Jesus is the pioneer of our salvation. A pioneer goes ahead to clear a path for others to follow. There is a sense of adventure associated with the pioneer going where no one has gone before. Along with adventure it takes courage. The pioneer blazes a trail for others to follow. The pioneer is motivated by the conviction that there is a better place out there somewhere and will stop at nothing until it is found.

The author of Hebrews portrays Jesus as the pioneer who opens the way to God. In a sense, Jesus broke down the wall separating people from their God. People had been searching for a way to God. Through his life, death, and new life, Jesus clears the way for us to enter into a relationship with God. Jesus has truly gone where no one has gone before leading the way to God the Father. We discover through Jesus that God desires to be in relationship with us, "in bringing many children to glory."

It is through Jesus' life, death, and resurrection that he achieved the goal God set before him, making "the pioneer of their salvation perfect through sufferings." Perfection signifies completeness. Through his suffering and death Jesus Christ gained "glory" not for only himself but for "many children," in fact all people. Thanks to Jesus we can count ourselves as God's own children.

Through Jesus' life he has made a new future available for us. We may from time to time endure setbacks and suffering here on earth but thanks to Jesus we can look forward to a future where God has the last word for each one of us.

Another image the author of Hebrews employs is that Jesus is our brother. While Jesus is the Son of God he was also human, and he experienced everything we have growing up. As an infant he experienced his mother's love as she held him and cared for his every need. There was a close bond between Mary and Jesus built upon the foundation of love. As a young man Jesus would learn carpentry skills from Joseph. Jesus would work crafting wooden items for other people. Jesus experienced every emotion that we do. He knew what it felt like to be loved and also to fall out of favor with people. He must have felt disappointment, especially when his chosen disciples did not grasp his objective. Like us, he might even have felt discouraged from time to time. Jesus understands us because he shared all these experiences.

We can identify with someone who knows and understands what we experience. Jesus is not "ashamed" to call us his brothers and sisters. The author of Hebrews claims, "For the one who sanctifies and those who are sanctified all have one Father. For this reason Jesus is not ashamed to call them brothers and sisters." It is an act of grace to be included in God's family. Jesus blazed a path for us to follow that led to God. We follow Jesus down that path knowing that he experienced the wide range of emotions that we do. We identify closely with Jesus because he became one of us. That is the definition of incarnation.

Another image to consider is that Jesus is our liberator who came to set us free, "and free those who all their lives were held in slavery by the fear of death." Sometimes we find ourselves drawn into situations we would rather avoid. Many people struggle through various addictions and vices. People caught up in destructive addictions need the help and intervention of another to pull them through. Jesus our liberator set us free to start over again. Only Jesus has the power to break the hold of sin in our lives.

Through the crucified and risen Christ, God confronts evil with love. Jesus sets us free. "Therefore he had to become like his brothers and sisters in every respect, so that he might be a merciful and faithful high priest in the service of God, to make a sacrifice of atonement for the sins of the people."

Jesus as the high priest is a theme that the author of Hebrews develops further in his epistle. "Since, then, we have a great high priest who has passed through the heavens, Jesus, the Son of God, let us hold fast to our confession" (4:14). Jesus offers himself to us in love so that our relationship with God can be restored.

Kay was in the seventh grade when her father died. One week later Kay was back in school even though her life had been filled with the grief of losing her dad. That first day back Kay was called to the principal's office, "for a chat." Mr. Cook told her he knew how hard it was to lose a father, however, "the best way to work through grief is to reach out to others," he told her.

He invited her to join what he called; the "Subs for Santa" drive that collected food and toys for needy families within the school district. Kay joined six other students in mid-December to deliver presents and foods to area families. This was a wonderful experience for her and the other students. "Even though there were still plenty of presents and food in the van, the other students were dropped off at their homes," she remembers.

"We came to my house," Kay recalls, "and I wished Mr. Cook a Merry Christmas and ran inside." A few minutes later there was a knock on the door — it was Mr. Cook with food, toys, and other presents. The entire school had been collecting presents for Kay's family. Kay was so touched that she sat on the stair and cried.

Kay remembers that Christmas of being thankful to her school, "for showing my family the true meaning of Christmas." Years later she fondly retells this story to her own children. "Christmas is to remember first Jesus, second others, and last yourself," she says.[2]

We do not know what the future holds but thanks to Jesus, we know the one who holds the future. We might not have received everything that we wanted or maybe we feel that post-Christmas let down. However, we have the one thing we really need — Jesus Christ. Jesus is the one present that we do not need to return but can keep forever. Amen.

1. Maureen Dowd, "A Tale of Trigger," *New York Times*, December 26, 2007.
2. Kay Lynn, "The Gift," *Love Matters, Delilah* (Ontario Canada: Harlequin, 2008), pp. 48-49.

Christmas 2
Ephesians 1:3-14

Signed, Sealed, and Delivered

Praise God for all the wonderful things God has done in our lives and in our world! We continue to be filled with awe and wonder. Our fitting response is to sing praises to our God. Our favorite praise hymns and songs can transport us beyond our present situation into the very presence of God.

The early Christians experienced the presence of God through their worship and singing. It is commonly believed that the first chapter of Ephesians contains words and phrases from hymns and liturgy that would have been familiar to first-century Christians. The apostle Paul might very well have been quoting a favorite hymn when he penned these words, "Blessed be the God and Father of our Lord Jesus Christ, who has blessed us in Christ with every spiritual blessing in the heavenly places." God has blessed us in and through Jesus Christ. God will continue to bless us as we enter a new year.

As we examine Jesus' life and teachings we discover how much God loves each and every one of us. "For God so loved the world that he gave his only Son, so that everyone who believes in him may not perish but may have eternal life," Jesus said (John 3:16). No price would be too high for God to pay to restore our relationship with God, even if it meant sacrificing God's own Son. As we take down our Christmas decorations, packing them away for another year, we need to acknowledge that Jesus suffered and died upon the cross for our sins and the sins of the world. God then raised Jesus from the dead. Paul explains, "In him we have redemption through his blood, the forgiveness of our trespasses, according to the riches of his grace." Jesus removed the burden and restored our proper relationship with God.

Because we are "in Christ" we have the opportunity for a new beginning, a fresh start. Even when we make bad choices in our lives God loves us so much that we are given another chance. At the beginning of the New Year we can set out with new resolve to claim the life that is possible because of Christ.

Peggy Dimino was driving home on New Year's Day when she was cut off by another driver. Her car slammed into a barrier on the right side of the highway, spun, crossed three lanes, hit the median, and burst into flames.

Jorge Baez was behind her and saw the terrible accident. Immediately he stopped and with the assistance of another man pulled Peggy from the burning car moments before the car was engulfed in flames.

Peggy was seriously injured and was in a drug induced coma for nearly two months. During her recovery she began thinking about her life. She had experienced problems at work; she struggled financially, often fought with friends, and ended romantic relationships. She remembered having a disagreement with her sister the day before her accident. In the hospital she was feeling unlucky and at times angry and bitter over what happened to her. "I just let it go," she says, "I realized how lucky I was."

When she was able to return to her home she stated that she wanted to meet the men who came to her rescue and saved her life. She discovered that Jorge lived near her and with the help of a radio station she learned the identity of the second man, Brice DeMuro. They met on New Year's Day one year after the accident. They reflected on how their lives had been changed as a result of that night. Brice went home and decided to quit smoking. Jorge had not always done good things but vowed that he would change and make his family proud.

"I believe you were sent to give me a second chance," Peggy told her rescuers. "It's made me appreciate life and people around me," she claims. "It's a new lease on life."[1] God through Jesus Christ has given each one of us a new lease on life, a second chance.

In living out our faith we discover just how deep God's love is for us and all people. We belong to God in and through Jesus Christ. That designation cannot be taken away from us. No matter what we do or where we are we will forever be children of God. We learn that God "chose us in Christ before the foundation of the world to be holy and blameless before him in love." Before any of us were born, even before Adam and Eve, Abraham and Sarah, Moses and Miriam, Mary and Joseph, God had a divine plan that included all people. God chose each one of us, designating us as God's own children. God loves all people as God's own children.

We are able to celebrate our unity in Christ — in spite of our life experiences and cultural differences we are all one in Jesus. The first-century church struggled with accepting people from different backgrounds and cultures. Whatever divided people and erected walls in the past, Jesus Christ dismantles. All believers are one in and through Jesus Christ. Elsewhere the apostle Paul claims, "There is no longer Jew or Greek, there is no longer slave or free, there is no longer male and female; for all of you are one in Christ Jesus" (Galatians 3:28). All distinctions of time and culture are erased. We are all God's children. God, "destined us for adoption as his children through Jesus Christ" before the creation of the world. God loves us that much.

The Ephesians and other first-century believers might have felt marginalized and unimportant, put down and ignored, but they found themselves at the center of God's design because they belonged to the risen Christ. They were part of God's plan, "for the fullness of time, to gather up all things in him, things in heaven and things on earth."

With this knowledge we welcome and embrace all people especially those who have experienced brokenness as well as difficulties in their lives. We reach out with the love of God to those who through no fault of their own feel unloved.

We belong to God here and now and also in the future. "In Christ we have also obtained an inheritance, having been destined according to the purpose of him who accomplishes all things according to his counsel and will." We commonly understand an inheritance as money we receive from a parent or relative, or some property that we quickly convert to cash. However, in Paul's day an inheritance was typically received as land that was not under any circumstance to be sold or lost. The inheritance would always remain in the family. Having been delivered from slavery to sin and death through the power of the resurrection of Jesus Christ, Paul claims that we too are promised an inheritance. We have already obtained our inheritance. We belong to Jesus and nothing can ever take that distinction away from us!

We marvel at the knowledge that God claims us as God's own. God had a plan before the creation of the earth to bring salvation through Jesus to all people. We have many reasons to praise God, "so that we, who were the first to set our hope on Christ, might live for the praise of his glory."

Our response to all that God in Christ has done for us can be to live our lives as faithful disciples of Jesus Christ. "In him you also, when you had heard the word of truth, the gospel of your salvation, and had believed in him, were marked with the seal of the promised Holy Spirit." When we share the love of God with all people; we participate in projects to assist those in need and contribute our money to help other people. We reach out to our neighbors beside us and across the street. We show love and concern to all people, no matter if they have had different life experiences from us.

We give thanks for those special people in our lives who lived out their faith in a contagious way that led us to Jesus. Laura affectionately remembers the example of her grandmother. While growing up she would bake cookies with her grandmother. Specifically they would bake Christmas cookies. Laura remembers watching as her grandmother rolled out, then cut dough into shapes: angels, Santa Clauses, trees, snowmen, and a star. "I always went over to help Grandma decorate these tasty, delicious cookies," she explains, "and help her fill many containers with cookies to give to family and friends." People who received her grandmother's cookies always told her that they were the best sugar cookies they had ever eaten.

Laura watched as her grandmother would fill containers with her cookies and send some to the local hospice, the children's center, and several local nursing homes. Her grandmother was always willing to share with others. She gave away more cookies than she kept.

Her grandmother was an inspiration in her life. There were other times throughout the year when her grandmother along with others from her church would collect soap, clothing, and school supplies to help children and adults in distant corners of the world. She would make school kits complete with pencils, markers, erasers, and plastic scissors to send to needy children.

Laura claims that her grandmother "was one of the most important, as well as most interesting people in my life."[2] If we live out our faith in such a way, others will be drawn to Jesus.

Because we are loved by God we reach out with that same love to all those we encounter in our daily lives. We belong to God. Our status as God's own children is marked or sealed by the promise of the Holy Spirit. The first chapter of Ephesians concludes that Jesus Christ is in charge. When God raised Jesus from the dead, he was placed, "far above all rule and authority and power and dominion, and above every name that is named, not only in this age but also in the age to come" (v. 21). Christ is working, even now at the beginning of a new year, working to accomplish God's purposes, and seeing that God's will is done on earth. Amen.

---

1. Quick and Simple, December 25, 2007-January 1, 2008.
2. Laura "Grandma's Hands," *Love Matters, Delilah* (Ontario Canada: Harlequin, 2008), pp. 36-38.

Epiphany of Our Lord
Ephesians 3:1-12

The Light Has Come

As the Magi scanned the heavens they noticed a star brighter than all the others in the night sky. It caught their attention enough to warrant further investigation. They felt as though the star had a message for them. They would follow the star to see where it would lead them. Their journey would cover hundreds of miles as well as a considerable amount of time before they would meet the Christ Child. The star of Bethlehem announced the birth of the Son of God to the world. The Magi were the first outsiders to respond by worshiping the newborn king.

Jesus Christ is the Light of the world. God's plan of salvation, long devised, has now been revealed to all people. The Light of Christ embraced the apostle Paul. In his letter to the Ephesians, Paul reminds them of his "commission of grace" to proclaim the good news of Jesus Christ to the Gentiles, those outside of Jewish circles. His epiphany came from divine revelation. Paul who once breathed fire persecuting believers would now spend the rest of his life sharing the gospel with all people.

The mystery once hidden is now out in the open for the entire world. Jesus Christ, God's Son, has come to bring salvation to all people. Paul writes, "In former generations this mystery was not made known to humankind, as it has now been revealed to his holy apostles and prophets by the Spirit." Once the people lived in darkness, unaware of God's grace, but now thanks to God sending Jesus, we live in the light.

It is truly amazing, that God's plan of salvation would include all people. God has acted, Paul informs his readers, so that "the Gentiles have become fellow heirs, members of the same body, and sharers in the promise in Christ Jesus through the gospel." All of God's promises including the convent made to Abraham and Sarah could now be claimed by the Gentiles. Through Christ they could claim the same inheritance as their Jewish sisters and brothers. They became heirs, members of the same body of Christ. This is truly amazing, even astonishing good news.

There are times in our own lives when we feel down and out. There are times when we struggle over employment or relationship issues. At other times it is health concerns that weigh us down. In those moments it would serve us well to take a breath and remember that we are members of God's own family. We are strengthened by the knowledge that God loves us so much that God sent Jesus, the Light of the world, to guide us. God in Christ will never desert us. The Ephesians to whom Paul was writing might have viewed themselves as insignificant and unimportant in God's grand scheme of things, but now they could make an amazing claim — they were a part of God's own family. They could now stand on the promises made to Abraham and Sarah, and Moses and Miriam. It was a mystery that has now been solved and explained. It was a mystery the people could now embrace. In previous ages this mystery was not revealed but now the secret is out. Epiphany is about sharing the Light of Christ with a world darkened by violence, crime, and broken lives.

Bernard describes himself as a man wandering through life with no grounding in a faith community. His family stopped attending church when he was in elementary school. As a young adult he was well paid in a distasteful profession that has "only a negative impact on the world." Barnard enjoyed financial success, but deep down was ashamed of his work. When he and his girlfriend, Catherine, had a son, the birth inspired him to seek a "meaningful positive life." The couple began looking for a church home in their community.

How do you think people in most churches would react to an unmarried couple with a baby, who benefited financially from an unsavory occupation? Fortunately the church welcomed them with open arms and did not judge them harshly. They felt loved in that congregation and soon began taking the steps to join the church.

The church required attending classes that Bernard and Catherine at first found intimidating. They continued to feel a sense of shame but committed themselves to the process. They became more than members of the church, their lives were transformed in authentic Christian community. Bernard says that he found "new perspectives, role models whose example of faith and Christian life" taught him that change was possible. They experienced the love and mercy of God, learned the Bible, prayer, and sang new songs of faith. Bernard and Catherine were married. Bernard reflects, "If we know God will forgive us, we can begin to forgive ourselves." Sensing a call to help others, Bernard quit his job and found a job where he serves people.[1]

Sometimes we in the church are guilty of conveying an attitude that we are better than other people. This attitude turns off would-be believers. Paul, however, was clear about his role, identifying himself as a "servant according to the gift of God's grace." Jesus reminds us, "The greatest among you will be your servant" (Matthew 23:11). Paul knew his place when he makes the claim that he was, "a prisoner for Christ Jesus, a servant according to the gift of God's grace." He also viewed himself as the "very least of all the saints." In another letter Paul claims to be the "the least of the apostles, unfit to be called an apostle, because I persecuted the church of God" (1 Corinthians 15:9). In all we do and say we must point the way to Jesus — the true light, and not to ourselves.

There was a time in Paul's life when he persecuted Christians. Filled with rage and zeal he set out to rid the world of believers. His entire life was changed after his encounter with Jesus Christ — the Light of the world. Whenever Paul preached or wrote to churches, he always acknowledged God's amazing grace in his own life.

As a result of his encounter Paul understood his new mission as bringing the gospel to the Gentiles and "to make everyone see what is the plan of the mystery hidden for ages in God who created all things." Paul passionately embraces this new direction in his life, even though he knew it would not be easy. There were times when the other apostles stood in opposition to him. At other times physical harm came to Paul because he proclaimed the good news of Jesus Christ. In the first verse Paul writes as a "prisoner for Christ Jesus." Paul would be arrested and placed in prison but his only crime was his love and devotion to the Lord Jesus. Nothing would stop Paul from sharing the gospel.

We are servants of Jesus Christ, knowing that we belong to him can give each one of us boldness and confidence as we live out our faith. Paul claims that "we have access to God in boldness and confidence through faith in him." Because of our status as God's own children that can never be taken away from us, we can live triumphant lives in Jesus Christ. As the church we are members of the body of Christ; we have a responsibility to share the good news of our faith with others, "with boldness and confidence." The season of Epiphany is about telling everyone about Jesus Christ, the Light of the World.

A church conducted a demographic study of their community. The findings surprised the congregation; there were a lot of low-income working single mothers with children living near the church. The leaders of the church met to brainstorm creative ways to reach out to these families. Someone suggested holding a movie night in the church, noting that low income people do not have a lot of discretionary money for such things. They could use their new video projector to show movies in fellowship hall on Friday nights.

Another person suggested that they rent one of those big lighted signs and place it in front of the church to advertise free movie night. Someone else said that they will need food for the children and parents that come. Across the street from the church was a pizza shop. Several members approached the owner, they told their idea to reach out to people in their community. They proposed that if they promised to buy all their pizzas from him, would he sell them at half price?

The pizza shop owner thought it was a great idea to provide a fun evening to families in the community. He proposed that if they placed the name of his shop on the sign in front of the church he would give them all the pizzas they wanted for free. The sign in front of the church was changed to read "free movie night Friday pizza provided by Fred's Pizza."

The first Friday night was a success, more people came to enjoy a movie and pizza than they ever expected. The pizza shop owner was also impressed. He told the church leaders that if they would print a flyer advertising Friday night movies and pizza he would include it with every take out pizza for the next three months free of charge. Thousands of families would be reached. These were the very people the church needed to reach. Research reveals that people age 18 to 45 order pizza at least once a week.

The children who enjoyed the free movie and pizza on Friday nights began attending Sunday school classes; a support group was formed for single mothers, who also began attending worship. That church had been experiencing a decline in membership and attendance for years but now was beginning to grow.[2]

What are some creative ways that we can reach out "with boldness and confidence" to people who are living in our community but do not yet know Jesus?

The mystery long hidden was made known to Paul that included the Gentiles and all people. The mystery is made known so that the church of Jesus Christ will prevail. Groups of believers would gather and form the church, "so that through the church the wisdom of God in its rich variety might now be made known to the rulers and authorities in the heavenly places." Nothing will or can stop the church. There might be times when the church loses its focus momentarily, but God always sends people to reform the church. The church of Jesus Christ continues in strength as it has for 2,000 years.

What once was a mystery has now been made known. Jesus the Light of the world has come. We share that light, the good news of the gospel with others "in boldness and confidence through faith in him." We've a story to tell to the nations and it begins where we live. Amen.

---

1. Diana Butler Bass, *Christianity for the Rest of Us* (San Francisco: HarperSanFrancisco, 2006), pp. 219-220.
2. "Becoming a Welcoming and Inviting Church" workshop by Reverend Larry Homitsky, 2008.

The Baptism of Our Lord
Epiphany 1
Ordinary Time 1
Acts 10:34-43

Spirit-Direct

"Growing up," Valerie recalled, "I was involved in many of my church's activities for children." Recently she returned to her home church and attended an adult Sunday school class with her parents. The class included members who were active in the church while she was growing up. Many of them greeted her and reminisced about her childhood. A man stood up during the announcements and said, "We'd like to welcome Valerie to our class. Remember," he added, "we helped train and teach her."

After this experience Valerie thought of the congregation's response following baptisms: "With God's help we will proclaim the good news and live according to the example of Christ." This man's words were true. Forty years ago at Valerie's baptism those church members made this promise and they kept it.

"Now that baptism promise has new meaning for me," she says. "Whether I'm helping with Vacation Bible School or teaching a class for children, I do so with more enthusiasm. Something I say or do may contribute to the spiritual growth of a child."[1]

We are reminded of the importance of our baptism and also our responsibility. When a child is baptized the congregation pledges to do all they can to help raise the child in the Christian faith. When adults are baptized the congregation also pledges their support.

This morning we celebrate the Baptism of our Lord Jesus Christ. We remember how he was baptized by John the Baptist in the Jordan River. Jesus' baptism was the starting point of his ministry, as it is for all Christians. Jesus would call his twelve disciples and embark on a mission that would forever change the world. We are here because Jesus' mission and ministry have touched us. We are here to continue the ministry that Jesus began long ago. We are Jesus' modern-day disciples.

Peter was changed as a result of his encounter with Jesus. A fisherman turned disciple and later apostle who would take the gospel to all people. We might not readily identify with Peter; however, we are probably more like him than we would care to acknowledge. Peter had moments when he clearly did not understand Jesus or his mission. There were times when he failed Jesus. Once Peter received the Holy Spirit there would be no stopping him and the other apostles as they proclaimed the good news.

Like many of us Peter had a hard time accepting change. He was set in his ways, having a clear sense of what was right and proper as far as his faith and practice were concerned. Jesus instructed his followers to go into the entire world to tell people about him. At first Peter was reluctant to go to Gentile lands. The idea of speaking with a Gentile or entering a Gentile's home made Peter feel quite uncomfortable. It was hard to overcome such strong feelings, especially something that went against everything he had always accepted and believed. Sometimes our faith requires that we stretch in new ways often pushing us out of our comfort zones.

So what did Peter do? One night Peter had a vivid dream, a powerful vision that would forever change the direction of his ministry. "He saw the heaven opened and something like a large sheet coming down, being lowered to the ground by its four corners." Further God instructed him, "Get up, Peter; kill and eat." Peter protests, "By no means, Lord." Peter was not sure what to make of this vision that went against what he believed concerning clean and unclean animals. He was open to the leading of the Holy Spirit. It was while he was puzzled that a Gentile man named Cornelius appeared. Isn't it amazing how God can bring people into our lives that impact us in unusual ways at just the right time? Frequently it is people that we do not even know that enter our lives causing us to rethink our position. Was Peter's vision about food or about people?

Peter did something he had never considered doing in his entire life, he entered a Gentile's house. Once inside he discovered that there were other Gentiles present in the house. They were eager to hear what he had to say. "You yourselves know that it is unlawful for a Jew to associate with or to visit a Gentile," Peter explained to his audience, "but God has shown me that I should not call anyone profane or unclean." Peter experienced a change of heart toward those outside of Jewish circles. He realized that it was the hand of God leading him to take the gospel to the next level, to the Gentiles and to all people. It is "God working in our hearts that produces change in our lives."

As our lesson from the Acts of the Apostles opens Peter is giving a sermon in Cornelius' house. His audience was eager to hear what he had to say. Peter told them, "I truly understand that God shows no partiality, but in every nation anyone who fears him and does what is right is acceptable to him." This was a radical departure for Peter to believe that, "God shows no partiality" but loves all people and that Jesus Christ is "Lord of all." Everyone, no matter what ethnic or cultural background, can call on the name of the Lord Jesus and be saved. This was a tremendous leap of faith for Peter that went against everything he had previously believed.

Jesus came preaching peace, Peter informed his captive audience. The message spread and now included all people. In his message, Peter made reference to John the Baptist baptizing Jesus, the only time this episode was mentioned outside of the four gospels. "How God anointed Jesus of Nazareth with the Holy Spirit and with power," Peter explained, "how he went about doing good and healing all who were oppressed by the devil, for God was with him." It was at Jesus' baptism when he received power from the Holy Spirit and inaugurated his ministry. God "anointed Jesus of Nazareth with the Holy Spirit." Peter and the others were eyewitnesses to Jesus' ministry. Peter retold the story of how sinful humanity put Jesus to death but that was not the end of the story as, "God raised him on the third day and allowed him to appear." The weeks following Easter the risen Jesus met with his apostles. Peter continued his message, "He commanded us to preach to the people and to testify that he is the one ordained by God as judge of the living and the dead." And that was exactly what Peter and the others were doing.

When we are open to the leading of the Holy Spirit and do what Jesus calls us to do God will bless our efforts, in amazing ways that frankly we might not ever have imagined. As Peter was wrapping up his sermon there in Cornelius' house, "the Holy Spirit fell upon all who heard the word." They were baptized "in the name of Jesus Christ." That day those outsiders became believers. For as Peter told them, "God shows no partiality," but welcomes everyone.

Deanna considered herself "skeptical bordering on cynical, an unlikely candidate for organized religion." When she began attending church the congregation welcomed her warmly and invited her into the adult inquirers' process. "I need fellow travelers to teach me," Deanna remembers, "to hold my hand, and to remind me of Jesus' promises." She embarked on a pilgrimage where she would encounter Jesus. Through the class she learned new ways to pray, how to read the Bible, all along enjoying being part of a community of faith. "I found a way to a heavenly father and divine family," was how she describes the process.

Although her parents could not remember, Deanna persisted in her quest to find out if she had ever been baptized.

She tracked down distant relatives, made dozens of phone calls, and finally located the church that her grandmother had belonged to when she was a baby. The church secretary told her that the baptismal records had been destroyed in a fire. Deanna was disappointed. However, three weeks later the church secretary called back to say that she had tracked down other records and that Deanne had indeed been baptized. "I was overjoyed," she recalled, "I was a child of God all along and I didn't know it."[2]

Think for a moment of the people that God has brought into your life. Some might be long-time friends while others you might have just met. What would it take to reach them with the life-saving gospel? What specific things could you do? Sometimes as Peter discovered we might need to change our attitudes before we are able to reach them. But like Peter we must be open to the leading of the Holy Spirit to welcome people into our fellowship who might have different life experiences. The question remains: Is God converting a Gentile into the community of faith or is God converting Peter to seeing new possibilities for mission? Actually the answer is both.

There are people we come in to contact with every day who do not have the slightest understanding of the Christian faith yet feel God's tug on their heart. Cornelius felt God's presence but needed Peter's direction. He and the others needed Peter to welcome them with open arms into the community of faith. Who are the people who will need our guidance as they come to faith?

"Everyone who believes in him receives forgiveness of sins through his name," Peter reminds us. Everyone! Amen.

---

1. Valerie Battle Kienzle, "This Promise" (Upper Room), November 1, 2004.
2. Diana Butler Bass, *Christianity for the Rest of Us* (San Francisco: Harper San Francisco, 2006), p. 64.

Epiphany 2
Ordinary Time 2
1 Corinthians 1:1-9

The Church Is the Place

The internet has changed the way people relate to each other. There now are a multitude of websites where people tell of their personal experiences, seek answers to their questions, or seek help for their problems. There are discussion forums where people can comment on anything and everything from politics and religion to personal relationships. People relate to another person's struggles and hope to find the advice or insight they desire. New communities are formed with people on various websites.

Nana claims that she was feeling far from God. She was seeking advice for ways to feel close to God. She told how she grew up in a Christian home but by her own admission during her freshmen year she began hanging out with "the wrong crowd" and began drinking. During that period she did not think about God at all. When she realized the error of her way she returned to her home church. Unfortunately, she did not feel welcome because, "everyone knows how I used to be," she explains. She is thinking about joining a new church where she could experience a fresh start. What advice would you offer?

She received several helpful responses. One person compared her situation with a child who makes a mistake. The writer claims that a parent does not stop loving a child because the child messed up. Hopefully the child learns from their mistake. Another person wanted to assure Nana that God still loves her. She was reminded that the church is a place for sinners, "no one there has the right to judge you," the person wrote so, "hold your head high."[1]

While the internet has changed the way people communicate with each other, one thing that has not changed is our human need to interact with other people. In days past people would write letters. Much insight is gained from reading a famous person's letters containing their thoughts over a long period of time.

When the Corinthian church began experiencing problems they wrote to the apostle Paul seeking his advice and hoping that he could offer solutions to their present difficulties. Reading Paul's letters is like reading someone's mail, or listening to a one-sided telephone conversation. While we do not know the specifics of the problems they were experiencing we can glean insight from Paul's response. It is also obvious that Paul loved and cared deeply for the people in that faith community. It must have broken his heart when he learned of the problems the Corinthians were experiencing.

The Corinthian congregation presented the apostle Paul with several major challenges. It is commonly believed that Paul spent a year and a half in Corinth. During that time Paul preached and taught about Jesus Christ. As people were converted to the Christian faith a church was started that met regularly for worship. Once the church was established it was time for Paul to move to another city to begin the process all over again.

Corinth was a thriving economic center inhabited by people from all over the Mediterranean world. Corinth was also a major port city that was filled with all sorts of vices. There were people who were well off and others who were poor. It does not take too much imagination to realize that amid such diversity, problems would soon ensue within that church.

Serious problems arose that threatened their unity and purpose. There was one group of people within the church who thought too highly of themselves. They thought they possessed superior spiritual gifts that in their mind made them better than everyone else. The result was that feelings were hurt, sides were drawn, and conflict erupted within the church. When problems arose the leaders wrote to Paul hoping that he could solve their dilemma and set them back on course.

Paul always affirmed the people who were dealing sensitively with the issues at hand. Paul's goal was always to build up the church and never tear it apart. In the first verse we discover that Paul was clear about who he was and what his mission was. Paul was called by God to be an apostle, a missionary to the Gentiles. His mission in life was to proclaim the good news of Jesus Christ to as many people as he could. That powerful vision would take Paul to places he never dreamed of going. Following the prompting of the Holy Spirit, Paul found himself in situations that he had never thought possible.

In the opening of his letter Paul mentioned the name of another man, Sosthenes. While we do not know much about Sosthenes, we do know that he was the former leader of the Corinthian synagogue who at one time filed charges against Paul. Paul's preaching is credited with winning him over to Christ. Two to four years later he was assisting Paul in his missionary activity. Sosthenes was by Paul's side in Ephesus as Paul penned his letter.

Paul mentioned this man's name to remind his readers that God has been at work among them and that even former adversaries can come to a saving knowledge of Jesus Christ. Even opponents can become friends because of their common devotion to Jesus Christ. Sometimes we are too quick to write someone off, saying such things as "that person will never change," when in reality God has been at work in that person's life. The time might come when that person accepts Jesus as Lord and Savior and changes. Paul no doubt shared with the Corinthians his own experience as a persecutor of the church and how his life was changed once he encountered the Lord Jesus who called him to preach the good news.

From that experience Paul was called to be an apostle. In the same way the Corinthians were chosen by God and called to be "saints." "To the church of God that is in Corinth," Paul wrote, reminding them that they were special, called by God to be saints. Even though they were experiencing some differences of opinion Paul was reminding them that they needed to continue working together to accomplish God's desire and purpose. They needed to pause to see the bigger picture of what God was calling them to do and cease their petty disputes.

We today are part of the body of Christ. We too are called by Jesus, to be the church. The church is the extension of the ministry that Jesus began. We became the hands and feet of Jesus going places and doing ministry that Jesus would do. We care for the "least of these" who are members of Jesus' family. We speak words of assurance to those who are confused or who struggle with issues of faith as Jesus would.

Sometimes we lose sight of the purpose of the church when we think it is all about us, our personal likes and dislikes, when in fact the church is called by God. The church primarily exists for the sake of others who do not yet know Jesus as their Lord and Savior. Like the Corinthians we need to work through our disagreements toward a common goal. God has called us together at this unique moment in time for a reason. Paul uses the word, "sanctified," which means set apart for God's holy purpose. We are set apart and marked as God's own people. We are here for a reason; we have much work to do. There are people who need to know Christ.

We need to join with other believers, "who in every place call on the name of our Lord Jesus Christ, both their Lord and ours." Our identity is formed not by looking at ourselves but by God through Jesus Christ. Within this larger context whatever disagreements we might have had will fade away as we become excited about our mission and ministry.

In spite of their problems Paul sincerely gave thanks to God for them. "I give thanks to my God always for you because of the grace of God that has been given you in Christ Jesus." Paul was able to thank God for the people in that community of faith, for all their prayers and gifts. Paul offered a prayer of thanksgiving to God for each person in that church. When we do not see eye to eye with another person we need to follow Paul's example and pray for them, thanking God for their witness.

We experience God's grace in our lives when we first respond to Jesus' call upon our lives. Grace also continues to sustain us in our daily walk with Christ. God's grace has a transforming element to it, working in our lives to draw us closer to Jesus. Grace can change and transform our lives making us more and more like Jesus each and every day.

Paul assured the congregation that they had indeed "been enriched in him, in speech and knowledge of every kind…" God had given the people everything they needed to be in ministry, they had all the gifts they needed as Paul wrote, "You are not lacking in any spiritual gift." However, spiritual gifts were misunderstood and even abused in that church by some who thought too highly of themselves and viewed them as a means to for their own personal edification. They momentarily forgot that all spiritual gifts come from God and are not of our own device but are meant to be shared within the congregation and used to build up the church.

What Paul wrote to the Corinthians could very well be said to us, we have all the gifts we need to be in ministry in our community. The focus then becomes on discovering and using our God-inspired gifts in concert with other believers to build up the body of Christ, the church. This will lead to the transformation of our community, nation, and ultimately our world. We need to remain focused on what we are as the church, keeping our vision and mission ever before us.

Our strength and endurance for ministry comes from our Lord Jesus. Paul assures us that Jesus, "will also strengthen you to the end..." The church has talented, committed, gifted people, so the question becomes what is preventing us from becoming all we can be?

Like countless others, Athena Dean was consumed by worldly success. She admits that she was using her talents to encourage people to make money rather than inspire them to a closer walk with Jesus. She became possessed with making more and more money to the extent that her religious routine had been on automatic pilot. She described her faith as a quick prayer and a few minutes glancing at a Psalm. "I couldn't remember the last time I'd heard God's voice," she acknowledged. She was earning more money than she had ever dreamed possible.

Then one weekend she was alone in her house and felt an overwhelming urge to pray. God began to show her that she had been using her God-given abilities to motivate people for the wrong ends. The next week she attended a leadership conference but as people spoke she realized how far she had strayed from where God wanted her to be. She prayed, "God, forgive me for being so deceived!"

Athena told her business associates that she was finished. She never again wanted anything in her life that was not God's will. With that she started a new business venture that allowed her to spend more time with her family. She began using her spiritual gifts at church on various ministry projects. God continues to work in her life. Today Athena has chosen to be consumed by God's Spirit and by doing God's will. "There's no question in my mind I've made the right choice," she says with confidence.[2]

Paul reminded the troubled Corinthians that even in the face of frustration, or failure, or faithlessness, God remains faithful. Paul states, "God is faithful; by him you were called into the fellowship of his Son, Jesus Christ our Lord." Our faithlessness cannot and will not cancel out the faithfulness of God! God is always faithful! Whatever difficulties the Corinthians were experiencing God's grace would see them through. The same is true for us — we are under-girded by God's grace in all that we do. Amen.

---

1. Christian Fellowship and Prayer Forum, www.web-church.com/christian-forums.
2. Athena Dean, "Consumed by Success," *Today's Christian Woman*, January/February 1997, Vol. 19, No. 1, page 30.

Epiphany 3
Ordinary Time 3
1 Corinthians 1:10-18

Divided We Fall

The power of a vision can transform people. We just celebrated Martin Luther King Day. Dr. King's "I have a dream" speech spoken on the steps of the Lincoln Memorial in Washington, DC, captivated the entire nation. He longed for the day when the color of a person's skin no longer mattered. We continue to be diligent in combating the sin of racism in fulfilling that vision. Powerful God-inspired visions can and do change people.

A passionate sense of mission and vision should motivate everyone within the church. Wonderful ministry can happen when everyone is working together, on the same goals, all for the glory of God. Unfortunately we know what can happen when people do not work together, or see eye to eye. "United we stand, divided we fall," were words of a popular folk song in the 1960s. There is much truth in that song, united together we can accomplish great things, but divided we fail.

"It all started long before I came," said Pastor Jason Kirk, pastor of the fictional Clyde's Corner Church. The founder of Clyde's Corner, Cedric Clyde, was a successful farmer at the turn of the twentieth century. To show his thanks to God, he paid for building the church. Just before he died, Cedric donated furniture to the church including, "a giant red horsehair couch whose rich color Cedric fancied would brighten the church." The horsehair couch was placed behind the pulpit. The huge chair featured massive curved arms with dark mahogany legs, each carved like the claw of a lion.

As the years passed, the church as well as the community changed, and that couch became the subject of a bitter dispute. Members of the Clyde family wanted to keep the couch where it was, while newer members thought the couch did not belong in the sanctuary. This debate sparked tension between the established members and the newer families who had moved to the country to get their children away from the drugs that were spreading into their suburban neighborhoods. The new families had bought up foreclosed farms and built beautiful homes in the hills. They were accustomed to fine furnishings, and they detested what they had dubbed, "the Victorian Leviathan" that dominated what otherwise was a plain church building.

However, the Clyde family viewed the couch in a different light. Their farms had fallen on hard times. They looked at the couch each Sunday and fondly remembered that their great-grandfather Cedric had founded the church. Although their tractors were rusting in the front yard, at least the pastor sat on Cedric's couch.

"Every sentence I put in the air," Pastor Kirk says of his sermons, "I see them all weighing whether it is ammunition for their side or the other side. Here I am preaching about the love of God, and everything I say is filtered through a single question: 'Is the pastor in favor of the red horsehair couch, or is the pastor against the couch?' "[1] On the surface this issue seemed insignificant but it was tearing the church apart. What suggestions would you offer to resolve this issue?

Our epistle lesson reveals some of the problems that the Corinthians were experiencing. The situation had reached the critical stage. People within the church were quarreling among themselves. What started as a simple disagreement now escalated into a full-scale conflict. Sides were taken. Harsh words were spoken. Some of the people might even have left the church. Given the current state of conflict the church was no longer attracting new people. Who would want to be drawn into a church conflict where they are immediately forced to take sides? When conflict rears its ugly head the mission and ministry of the church comes to a grinding halt. The final result is that nothing much gets accomplished.

In the midst of these very serious problems the apostle Paul was contacted. Paul was the founding pastor of the church. The people were confident that Paul would be able to advise them and help them work through the problems that threatened the future existence of the church. Through correspondence Paul was made aware of the situation. Paul's goal was to always build up the church and never tear it down. With a pastor's heart Paul wrote to his former congregation, "Now I appeal to you, brothers and sisters, by the name of our Lord Jesus Christ, that all of you be in agreement and that there be no divisions among you, but that you be united in the same mind and the same purpose."

The issue that was tearing the church apart could not continue but needed to end as soon as possible. Resolution was needed. Paul was trying to recapture the passion that the people held for their church when he was with them. Paul wrote, "That all of you be in agreement." Instead of focusing on their differences, on what was tearing them apart, Paul was trying to rekindle their earlier passion. What brought them together in the first place was their love of the Lord Jesus, their sense of mission in reaching out and caring for the needs of others in that community united them. What united them was more powerful than what pulled them apart.

Sometimes we have to go back to the beginning, our mission and purpose, before we are able to move forward. It was time for the Corinthians to refocus. They needed to realize that there was more that united them than divided them. "Be in agreement," Paul pleaded, "that there be no divisions among you, but that you be united in the same mind and the same purpose." At one point in their journey they claimed Jesus Christ as their Lord and Savior. In the early days of the church the people were united in their mission and ministry.

Paul was calling to the people to remember who they were and more importantly to whom they belonged.

There will be times when there will be disagreements among members of the church. There will be times when people do not see eye to eye and that is all right. From time to time there are issues that find people on opposite sides — again that is all right. We still must love and respect each other. We are united in our ministry and mission.

Paul was not urging uniformity, but rather celebrating our God-given gifts. God made us all different. Diversity within the congregation is a good thing, something to be celebrated, and not a cause for strife.

Later in 1 Corinthians, Paul compares the human body with the church, the body of Christ. Just as the human body has various parts, each performing different functions, so too does the church. Every believer has a God-inspired gift. We do not all have the same gifts, and we need not feel badly because someone else has different gifts. When we use our gifts together, united in our mission and purpose, we make a whole. The church would be a boring place if everyone was alike and thought the same way. Too much sameness would make it difficult to fulfill the mission and ministry of the church. God created us all to be different.

Following Paul the next pastor had different gifts; he might have been a better preacher. There were some in that congregation who in effect began following Apollos while others remained loyal to their former pastor claiming, "I belong to Paul." Still others said, "I belong to Cephas," or "I belong to Christ." We know Cephas as the apostle Peter. It is interesting that Peter is mentioned since there is no evidence that Peter ever visited Corinth. Nonetheless, there were some who claimed loyalty to Peter; others to Apollos and others to Paul. The situation was getting out of hand. A sure fire way to destroy a church is to break into divisive cliques. United we stand, with everyone working together toward the same goals. Divided we fall, breaking into divisive factions. There is no room in the church for such nonsense. The ministry and mission of the church will suffer when conflict cannot be resolved in a timely fashion.

The situation in the Corinthian church had to stop immediately, the mission and ministry of the church was at stake. Paul asked a series of rhetorical questions, "Has Christ been divided? Was Paul crucified for you?" The obvious answer to all of Paul's questions is "no, of course not!" Paul wanted the people to see the absurdity of the situation.

Paul clearly knew what gifts he possessed and his mission, as he writes, "For Christ did not send me to baptize but to proclaim the gospel, and not with eloquent wisdom, so that the cross of Christ might not be emptied of its power." The Lord Jesus sent Paul to preach the gospel, not with "eloquent wisdom" nor to baptize converts, but to proclaim the good news of Jesus Christ.

United we stand! There is no telling what the church will accomplish with everyone working together for the common good, with a clear sense of vision and mission. When that unity of purpose does not exist, the church will falter and fall into petty quarreling. The ultimate result will be that the mission of the church will be sidetracked and nothing much will be accomplished. Divided we fail!

Back to the fictional church at Clyde's Corner, the one fighting over the giant red couch, a solution eventually was reached thanks to the leadership of its pastor. Everyone agreed that they needed to refurnish the parlor. The pastor pointed out that the couch was coming unglued and the veneers were splitting because of the extreme changes of temperature in the sanctuary. The pastor suggested having the couch repaired and placed in the parlor, which is kept at the same temperature all week with committee meetings almost every night.

The church rallied together. All of Cedric's relatives agreed with Pastor Kirk's plan and the new people donated money for the entire project, including the cost of framing a portrait of Cedric Clyde to hang over his couch. A cross was hung behind the pulpit. The Sunday of the dedication, Pastor Kirk preached on the cross and then added, "When we took the old couch out of the chancel we drove the bad feelings out, and the cross brought a new spirit in."[2] The church at Clyde's Corner had rediscovered its focus. Everyone's ideas and gifts were valued. Now the church could concentrate on its ministry and mission. Now the church could truly be the united body of Christ.

What are the red horsehair couches that are preventing us from rallying together to do the work of the church in our community? What is holding us back? There are people who are hurting who need to know Christ and the love and support of the church — people that we should be reaching.

May we continue to stand united in our mission and purpose as the church of Jesus Christ. We celebrate the gifts of each person who is part of our church family. To advance the mission of the church it takes everyone working together, not for personal recognition but for the glory of God. Amen.

---

1. Thomas H. Troeger, *The Parable of the Ten Preachers* (Nashville: Abingdon Press, 1992), pp. 20-22.
2. *Ibid*, pp. 93-96.

Epiphany 4
Ordinary Time 4
1 Corinthians 1:18-31

Lift High the Cross

There might be times in our lives when we are confused and unsure about what direction to go next. We live in the information age with readily available knowledge literally at our finger tips. There has been more information generated in the last thirty years than during the past 5,000. Having an abundance of information available does not always solve our problems. We are told that to improve our health we should try different foods, new drugs, or vitamin supplements, only to discover a couple of years later that we should avoid that particular product. Instead of being beneficial a new study reveals the product might actually cause harm. All this wealth of information leaves us confused.

We need to hear the apostle Paul's words whenever we are confused and mistakenly think that church is about us and meeting our immediate needs. Paul reminds us that not everything is about us. Paul draws our attention instead to the foundation of our faith.

As we have discovered the Corinthians experienced more than their share of problems before they contacted the apostle Paul with the hope that he could set them on the right path again. They had lost their focus and were reduced to fighting with each other. Sides were drawn and harsh words spoken. The inevitable result was feelings were hurt, and the mission of the church came to a grinding halt.

While there were some people within that church who were of noble birth, the majority were not. Those with this perceived higher status thought they were better than the other people. Others thought they possessed more knowledge or were on a higher spiritual plane than everyone else in the church. These attitudes were causing the problems within the church. Today we must constantly be on guard against having a superior attitude because we are church going people, believing that we are somehow better than other people who have had different life experiences and are not part of the church. If we are not careful the attitude that we are better than other people can creep into the church. The end result is instead of attracting people to Jesus Christ and the church those attitudes repel people, turning them off completely. Who can blame them for not wanting to have anything to do with the church?

In the midst of all this Paul goes back to the basics of our faith. At times when we lose our focus it is always good to review what we believe. While the people were divided into groups their common denominator was the cross. In the front of most churches is the cross. The cross reminds us that Jesus Christ suffered and died for our sins and the sins of the world. Furthermore, the cross symbolizes that God raised Jesus from the dead. Jesus Christ is the resurrected Lord in whom we place our trust. Paul wrote, "For the message about the cross is foolishness to those who are perishing, but to us who are being saved it is the power of God." There is power in the cross because it represents the power of God at work in our lives and in our world.

Paul knew the transforming power of the cross from his own personal experience. Earlier in his career Paul felt that he needed to persecute followers of Jesus. In his mind he believed that eliminating Christians was what God desired of him. All that dramatically changed after Paul's encounter with the risen Lord Jesus on the road to Damascus. Paul was struck blind for three days and when another believer touched him his sight returned. When he opened his eyes he viewed his faith differently, he came to grips with the transforming power of the cross of Jesus Christ. Instead of persecuting believers Paul became the church's foremost missionary.

Nothing would be able to stop Paul from proclaiming the good news of Jesus Christ.

Rick Founds works at a fiber optics company. On the weekends Rick is a worship leader at his church. Every morning Rick reads scripture on his computer monitor. Then, he says, "I'd just reach over and grab my guitar. I'd plunk along with whatever I was reading that day."

One morning, as he was studying the attributes of God, he began writing some notes when suddenly it struck him; "God knows the end from the beginning. God had a plan to redeem us from the very beginning." As Rick meditated over the morning's Bible verse and plucked his guitar he thought about the cycle of rain that comes down and waters the earth, then evaporates into the clouds, and then returns. Suddenly the now-famous chorus emerged, "You came from heaven to earth to show the way. From the earth to the cross, my debt to pay; From the cross to the grave, from the grave to the sky."

"Knowing the whole history of humanity, from its beginning to its end," Rick reflects, "God made the decision 'to show the way.' The response to grasping even a little bit of that knowledge can only be praise and thanksgiving and gratitude!"[1]

However, not everyone was drawn to the power of the cross. To those who sought after human wisdom the cross was viewed as a symbol of death and ultimately failure. Some people believed wisdom was the pathway to enlightenment and had difficulty focusing on the cross. The people living in Corinth were heavily influenced by Greek thought and philosophy. Paul points out that worldly wisdom did not lead to salvation, "the world did not know God through wisdom," Paul claims. All the wisdom in the world does not lead anyone to God. Only through the cross can we find the God who saves us.

A word of caution is in order; Paul was not saying that acquiring wisdom was not important. We benefit daily from the many scientific and medical advances made over the last fifty years. Many diseases have been eliminated through the hard work of dedicated doctors and researchers to which we are thankful. While learning is important we need to remember that knowledge does not always lead us to God.

Some viewed the cross as foolishness. The notion that God would save humanity through the cross was inconceivable to those from a Jewish background. They had preconceived notions of what the messiah would accomplish; the idea that the messiah would suffer and die was nonsense to them. They demanded a "sign." The Greeks loved wisdom and might not have given the cross a second thought. While the cross was a stumbling block and foolishness for some people, it was the power to save a sinful humanity. For that reason Paul proclaimed the cross.

Paul redefines wisdom as Christ for both Jew and Greek, "Christ the power of God and the wisdom of God." This serves as another reminder that God's ways are not always our ways. The way we look at our world is not the same way that God sees us. Paul explains, "For God's foolishness is wiser than human wisdom, and God's weakness is stronger than human strength."

It was time for the people to go back to the basics of faith. Paul wanted the people to "consider your own call." Not many were wise by human standards, or powerful, or of noble birth, but God called them to become the church — to witness to their community the good news of Jesus Christ. The power of the cross is that only God is able to take people who appear to be insignificant, or weak, and transform them. Paul was a living example of someone who underwent a major life transformation.

God is the source of all our human achievements. God deserves the credit. If we are going to boast, Paul suggests let us, "boast in the Lord."

Jane Johnson Struck experienced one of those uncomfortable Holy Spirit moments in church one Sunday. As she stood singing with the congregation, "I suddenly felt surprised by the chorus." She remembered being moved by the words, "I give my life to follow/ Everything I believe in/ Now I surrender."

While she had sung this song before the words impacted her in a fresh way that morning. She always assumed that the words alluded to person's whole-heartedly following their belief in Jesus Christ. However this time she felt a different emphasis as she sang those words. "It's about surrendering what I believe to truly follow."

"I believe and have accepted Jesus as my Savior and Leader," she claimed. Then she recalled a Bible study where they talked about the difference in "believing in God and believing God." She discovered that belief is always active. Her believing God should transform every aspect of her daily life as well as how she views others and the world.

For far too long Jane believed what she now labels as a lie, "I'm not as worthy of God's love as other Christians." To compensate for her perceived inadequacies she wrote, "I've tried to earn love by being nice — someone who's caring, and kind, sweet, who tries not to rock the boat or upset anyone." However, Jane realized that she needed to surrender this lie. "I cringe to think of the years I've allowed this faulty belief to influence me. "We're all equals at the Cross."[2]

It's easy to lose our focus and allow other thoughts to invade our faith. In order to surrender all to Jesus we might have to relinquish everything that gets in our way. Sometimes it is our attitudes that prevent us from becoming the people Jesus has called us to be. The Corinthians thought wisdom was the pathway to God. Instead, Paul wanted them to focus on the cross of Jesus Christ.

While the Corinthians were vying for positions of power and status Paul encouraged them to take a fresh look at the Cross and reconnect to the power of God at work in their lives. God chose people who were weak and powerless "so that no one might boast in the presence of God."

May we continue to focus on our Lord Jesus Christ. We are called together to be the church in our community. We surrender our lives to Jesus. Amen.

---

1. Phil Christensen & Shari MacDonald, "Lord, I Lift Your Name," Men of Integrity June 25, 2003.
2. Jane Johnson Struck, "The Lies I Believe," www.blog.christianitytoday.com/mt/mt-tb.cgi/2216.

Epiphany 5
Ordinary Time 5
1 Corinthians 2:1-12 (13-16)

Discerning in Love

Many people have come to rely on Global Positioning Systems (GPS) to travel from one place to another. GPS is especially helpful when you are traveling in an area that you are unfamiliar with. By typing in the address of your destination, the GPS will inform you where and when to turn. If you miss a turn it will recalculate your position and get you back on course. The GPS will get you to your destination in one piece and in the same condition you were in when you left.

While there is a definite advantage to traveling with such a device, GPS cannot help us navigate our faith and our relationships with each other. Love asks why we are in a particular place at a specific time. Sometimes the difficulties that we experience are because we do not pause to ask, "Why are we going there?" We should always be open at every moment to what God wants to teach us and lead us.

The problem is that there are so many distractions that lure us away from the faith. We often become lost when we follow too many detours. As we have discovered it did not take much for the Corinthians to become distracted and confused. The apostle Paul spent a year and a half teaching the Corinthians about Jesus and the Christian faith. Paul then set out for a new destination to begin the process all over again, witnessing to others about Jesus, and then starting a new church. It was not long after Paul left that the Corinthians began having problems. When they sought Paul's help and advice, he realized that the problems were serious enough that they threatened the church's very existence as well as their future.

Without the aid of a GPS, Paul determined that the people needed to go back to the beginning, to the foundation of their faith. When we lose our focus, we can get back on track by going back to the beginning — the basis of our faith. We gather this day and every Sunday because of what God has done and continues to do in and through Jesus Christ. It is easy to become confused and view our faith in terms of what benefits we personally receive. Paul brings us back hoping to rekindle the faith we once professed.

When Paul was with them he preached about the cross of Christ. He was both honest and humble in admitting that "I did not come proclaiming the mystery of God to you in lofty words or wisdom." His message was simple and to the point as he preached about Jesus Christ. Paul wanted the people to understand the power of God at work in and through Jesus Christ. Paul might very well have called attention to himself; after all he founded that church. However, he did not — instead he preached about the cross. "So that your faith might rest not on human wisdom but on the power of God," Paul wrote. Paul relied on the power of God to allow his own words to produce fruit. The success of the church does not rest on one individual but on the power of God, "with a demonstration of the Spirit."

As soon as Paul left Corinth other more polished, flashy speakers came and won a following among the people. It was then that Paul's preaching style as well as his message was criticized. With humility Paul acknowledged his own shortcomings and inadequacies. When he first spoke he did so with fear and trembling. Paul preached "nothing among you except Jesus Christ, and him crucified." Paul understood the danger of elevating the preacher to become the focal point of the message. The crucified Christ is the center of our faith.

Paul modeled the proper attitude for the troubled Corinthians. Paul never drew attention to himself or his many accomplishments or even mentioned that he founded the church in Corinth. He might have desired that the church be named after him, or that his name be placed everywhere as a constant reminder of his importance in the life of that congregation. But he did not. Instead he preached, "Nothing among you except Jesus Christ, and him crucified." Paul knew that the faith did not center on him but rather was all about Jesus Christ.

A serious threat to the unity and future of the church was a group of people who thought too highly of themselves. They viewed themselves as being wise. They incorrectly believed that they possessed superior spiritual gifts. Whenever anyone claims to be on a higher spiritual plane than others in the church there will always be hurt feelings. Paul skillfully called the congregation back to the foundation of their faith, the cross. In effect, it was time to review what they believed in and why they held those beliefs.

Paul preached Christ, "so that your faith might rest not on human wisdom but on the power of God." The message is that simple, although sometimes we are guilty of making it too complex for people to understand. Paul knew that the people who became believers did not do so because of him but rather through the power of God's Spirit at work in their midst. It was God's power that seized them and made them God's own people.

For over sixty years Billy Graham has preached the good news of Jesus Christ. Dr. Graham has preached before more people than anyone. With many of his crusades televised he has reached millions of people around the world. A couple of years ago Dr. Graham celebrated his ninetieth birthday. People were encouraged to write messages to the evangelist. Many gave moving testimonies of coming to faith during a particularly difficult time in their lives.

One person wrote, "I am grateful for the opportunity to tell you how God has used you in my life." He went on to tell of the time in 1995 when he was between combat tours of the Persian Gulf and Bosnia. One night he was sitting in the barracks "seriously contemplating suicide." He claims that a voice in his head told him to turn on the television. It was then that he discovered a televised crusade with Dr. Graham preaching. At one point in his message Dr. Graham said that we should not hurt ourselves and that suicide is not the answer.

"I was loved that night," the person writes, "I cannot put into words what the Lord did for me that night." He goes on to say that he has served the Lord Jesus ever since and is today involved in ministry to people who have experienced trauma. As he concludes his note of appreciation he writes, "with tears gushing from my eyes as I reminisce of all that has happened in my life as I have served the Lord, which all started that cold February night in northern Canada when I didn't take my life, but gave it to God."[1]

"For I decided to know nothing among you except Jesus Christ, and him crucified," Paul writes. We proclaim the good news and then rely on the power of God to transform lives.

Faith is grounded not on human wisdom or performance but rather on God's power. There is nothing wrong with learning, unless we use it to put other people down. Not everyone who claims to possess wisdom grasps God's wisdom. "We speak God's wisdom," Paul writes, "secret and hidden, which God decreed before the ages for our glory." No everyone understood God's purpose in sending Jesus, which is why the earthly rulers sentenced him to death. They might have thought they were doing what was right, but in fact they were opposing the will of God. In a sense Paul was telling his readers that although they thought highly of themselves for possessing human wisdom, they were in danger of opposing God.

God's plan was not revealed to those who considered themselves wise but rather to those who purposefully sought God's will. Those who were ready to listen for God's voice grasped God's intent. The ways of God are discernible when we allow the Holy Spirit to teach us God's ways. "These things God has revealed to us through the Spirit," Paul boldly states, "for the Spirit searches everything, even the depths of God." The Holy Spirit is at work in the lives of all believers. Later in his letter Paul writes about encouraging believers to use their spiritual gifts to benefit other people.

Within the Corinthian congregation were some who were critical of Paul's preaching, specifically for not instructing them in all aspects of wisdom. In his response Paul says that he did in fact teach wisdom but not everyone understood. Paul defines true wisdom as building up the church and seeking God's will in light of the cross of Jesus Christ. While the world might scoff at that notion it is, nonetheless, God's plan of salvation. This serves as another reminder that God's ways are not always our ways. What we think is important might not be so in God's eyes.

We relate to God not through wisdom but rather by love. We must strive to be more like Jesus and act and react as Jesus would. As spiritual people Paul claims that we have the mind of Christ. Bearing the mind of Christ should be evident in all that we do both as individuals and as the church.

Susan felt no real sense of direction in her life. She claims that this is due to always trying to please others. Other people were always making requests of her. She began to take daily walks where she listened for the voice of God and the guiding of the Holy Spirit. "I have to remove myself from the voices that barrage me in order to find my true compass," Susan explained.

"Discerning God's voice is not so hard when I make time to listen closely," she claimed. Sometimes it was a sudden insight, while at other times it was a sense of reordering her priorities or conviction about what she should say or do.

Her walks allowed her to slow down enough to listen for God's direction. She said that faith is about entering into a relationship with God through Christ and "not about intellectualizing God's commands, but internalizing his truth within my heart." This understanding affected not only her thoughts but also her actions.

"I am most at peace when I tune out the voices of the world long enough to hear the still, small voice of God directing me."[2]

In a church that was in danger of dividing, Paul preached that unity came from acknowledging the cross of Jesus Christ. When we look for unity in anything other than the cross of Christ we will become something other than the church.

We gather in worship each week to discern God's will for our lives, for our church, and for our world. There is a corporate nature to our faith. That is why it is important to worship together. We also seek God's will individually through our prayers, fasting, Bible readings, and other devotional readings. Our desire is to know God's will. Paul reminds us, "Those who are spiritual discern all things, and they are themselves subject to no one else's scrutiny." Amen.

---

1. www.BillyGraham90.com.
2. Susan Cosio is a chaplain at Sutter Medical Center in Sacramento, California, This I Believe.com.

Epiphany 6
Ordinary Time 6
1 Corinthians 3:1-9

Grow Up!

The best way to jump-start your spiritual life, according to a recent survey, is to serve others in Jesus' name, in addition to studying the Bible. Eighty thousand people from 200 churches responded to this survey. What sent shock waves to pastors and leaders everywhere is that the weekly worship service can only carry a person so far in aiding spiritual growth. If the person only attends worship after awhile they become bored, angry, and sometimes leave the church. They describe their experience as being stalled in their spiritual growth.

According to this extensive study, serving is the most catalytic experience in fostering spiritual growth. "It appears that serving experiences are more significant to spiritual development than organized small groups" was one of the conclusions from this study. Reaching out and serving other people in Jesus' name does more for our spiritual growth than anything else. Not to mention that in serving we are helping other people in Jesus' name.

Spending time reading and studying the Bible is another way to fuel your spiritual life. "Spending time in the Bible is hands down the highest impact personal spiritual practice... that is most predictive of growth." While attending weekly worship services is important, serving, and spending time in God's word will catapult people in their spiritual life.[1]

As modern-day disciples of Jesus Christ, we are called to live out our faith in practical ways. Jesus defined believers as, "the light of the world"(Matthew 5:14). Jesus instructs us to let our light shine for others to see and not keep it to ourselves. While we live in the world we are not of the world. When people see how we conduct ourselves on a daily basis it should be noticeably clear from our behavior that we are different from the rest of the world. The love, joy, and generosity in our lives should stand out. If we blend in with everyone else there would be reason for concern.

The Corinthian church presented quite a problem for the apostle Paul. Within that new church some people thought too highly of themselves, and this only added to their problems. Whenever there are people within the church who project themselves as better than everyone else there are bound to be problems as well as hurt feelings. Paul tried his best throughout his letter to point out the error of their ways with the hope that they would change.

In the previous chapter Paul wrote about wisdom, knowing that there were people within that church who thrived on wisdom. The danger was that a group of people thought they knew it all, or maybe that their understanding was greater than Paul's. Paul brought them back to reality when he wrote, "I could not speak to you as spiritual people, but rather as people of the flesh, as infants in Christ." This was not what they wanted to hear. They thought that they were mature believers, while Paul reminded them that they were still babes in Christ.

Paul uses the metaphor of an infant to describe how a person comes to faith. The new believer learns the basics of the faith: how God created the world, how Jesus suffered and died for all of our sins, and how the Holy Spirit empowers us for ministry. The starting point is entering into a relationship with Jesus Christ. The next steps would be reading the Bible, attending worship, and learning from other believers. These steps can be compared to the milk that nourishes infants. Just as an infant grows and begins to eat solid food so the believer should continue to grow and mature in the faith. The problem is that it does not always happen. People become stuck or stalled in their faith development. This was a problem in the

Corinthian congregation and is still a problem in many of our churches today as well.

The current spiritual landscape has been described as being a mile wide but only a half inch deep. The task of the church is to help people grow in their faith. One way is by providing instruction and resources. To make disciples we have to dig deep into God's Word. We have to step outside of our comfort zones and serve others in Jesus' name.

The danger is when we reach a point in our spiritual lives when we feel we no longer need to grow. That was the point Paul was trying to make to the Corinthians. The people stopped growing and were in effect stuck in infancy for far too long. They should have been eating solid food but were still only drinking milk. They should have been maturing in their faith but were behaving like babies. They should have been walking or learning to ride a bike but they were still crawling on their hands and knees — they were stuck! What made the situation worse was that the Corinthians did not realize they were stuck. They thought they were doing all right when in fact they were not. "Even now you are still not ready," Paul advised.

As long as there was division in the congregation they were not mature or growing in their faith. "For as long as there is jealousy and quarreling among you," Paul boldly wrote, "are you not of the flesh, and behaving according to human inclinations?" With their fighting, jealousy, and quarreling they were living like everyone else — like much of the world. As growing, maturing believers they should have out-grown such behavior. The way they treated each other in the church should have been noticeably different from the rest of the world. But unfortunately that was not the case.

Within the fellowship of the church there is no place for people to insist on their own way to the exclusion of everyone's ideas and feelings. Whenever people insist on their own way, they hold everyone else spiritually hostage to the detriment of the mission of the church.

Knitting groups have been started in many churches. Women come together to knit and pray together, sometimes reading out loud favorite verses or singing hymns. Most knit scarves, blankets, and baby clothes to give away. But often the creative act of crafting combined with the power of giving transforms women spiritually. Meetings become places of spiritual connection.

One group, which meets in a church in Chicago, call themselves "Crafty Angels" and focuses on serving the poor. What they make and give away is truly impressive. In 2006 the group donated more than 3,000 items including baby caps and blankets for a local hospital, hats, mittens, and scarves for a community outreach. They're also involved in "Afghans for Afghans," which collects hand-knitted blankets for a women's hospital in war-ravaged Afghanistan. The group that meets at the church is small, only ten in number but another fifty women from around the country stay in touch via email and send in items they have knitted.

"The women are thrilled to do something they love to make a difference," says one of the organizers, Chris Pokorny. "I enjoy telling them, 'You're helping people around the world.' It's exciting to see women empowered and mobilized. They realize they can do God's work through something they like to do." Then she adds, "That's energizing."[2] With everyone working together the church can do amazing things in the name of Jesus Christ.

Paul is credited as starting the church at Corinth, but another preacher Apollos came after he left. In that conflicted congregation sides were drawn with some remaining loyal to Paul and others claiming, "I belong to Apollos." It is dangerous to our spiritual health when we elevate pastors to that level, and it is also bad for the pastor. People become stuck when all they think about is a former pastor or how much better they like the new preacher than the previous one. Pastors are not in competition with one another.

Paul reminded the troubled Corinthians that both he and Apollos were on the same side. Each individual had different gifts, as Paul will claim later in his letter. When one person's gifts are used in conjunction with other gifts within the congregation the church will thrive.

Neither pastor tried to elevate himself either as Paul reminds his readers. Both were servants of the risen Lord. Paul viewed his role as planter, like a farmer who plants seeds, so Paul began the church. For growth or maturity to take place someone would have to water the seeds. In this case it was Apollos who followed Paul. But neither gentleman should have received credit or accolades because they were only fulfilling their God-given tasks. "God gave the growth," Paul and Apollos were both servants.

"So neither the one who plants nor the one who waters is anything, but only God who gives the growth," Paul stated. Unlike the people Paul was addressing in his letter, he sought no special status, nor was he in competition with Apollos or any other pastor. Their gifts were complementary. Paul allowed God to use him in any way that would benefit the kingdom. Apollos could not do what Paul did and Paul could not do what Apollos did — both used their God-given gifts to build up the church. Their efforts would not have amounted to much if it were not for God.

God can and will do amazing things in our lives and in the life of our church when we surrender our will to God's. "For we are God's servants, working together," we work together to the glory of God and not to receive human recognition or applause. This was what Paul hoped his friends in Corinth would soon understand. It was time for the Corinthians to grow up!

The church, just like the field in Paul's metaphor, belongs to God. Individual leaders who come and go are insignificant;

they are simply field hands. The church belongs to God. Amen.

---

1. Greg L. Hawkins and Callie Parkinson, Follow Me (Chicago: Willow Creek Association, 2008), pp. 40, 114.
2. Ken Wyatt, "Praying and Purling," Today's Christian Woman, Sept/Oct. 2007, Vol. 29, No.5.

Epiphany 7
Ordinary Time 7
1 Corinthians 3:10-11, 16-23

Building a Solid Foundation

The long-awaited dream would soon become a reality. Ground was broken for the family's new home. The ground was cleared and soon a foundation was dug; blocks and then cement were laid. Then masons came and carefully laid the bricks. Carpenters were next on the scene, nailing two-by-fours, framing the new house. After only a few weeks the house was beginning to take shape, which pleased the family. Roof trusses were carefully hoisted into place. Once the outside work was completed attention would be given to the interior of the house. Within a few short months the family would enjoy their new home. They could hardly wait.

What would happen if when the carpenters arrived they became jealous of the masons' work and in a fit of anger knocked down all the bricks? If when word reached the masons they too became enraged and destroyed all the carpenters' work, pulling down the frame of the house. Not only would the completion of the house be delayed, and the family would be disappointed, but in fact, the durability of the house would be in question. Who would want to live in such a house? The workers would have to return to redo the work they had already completed; it would cost them their time and any additional materials that were needed. What would happen if both offending parties would arrive at the same time to make repairs? It would not be inconceivable to see fist fights breaking out among the workers.

In effect, the Corinthians were experiencing that same sense of destruction within their congregation. Sides were drawn, harsh words were spoken, and the work and mission of the church came to a grinding halt. Paul's goal was always to build up the church and never tear it apart. When Paul heard what was taking place in the church, it must have broken his heart. He loved the Corinthians and certainly wanted the very best for the church that he founded. Paul's immediate goal was to restore order in the church so that the church could continue to be a beacon of hope and light in their community.

Paul claims, "Like a skilled master builder I laid a foundation, and someone else is building on it." During the eighteen months to two years that Paul was in Corinth, he purposefully set out to lay a solid foundation, knowing that others would come and build on what he started. Paul did not rely on his own knowledge as much as he rested on the grace of God to build a solid foundation, which he says, "is Jesus Christ."

Care along with maturity must be exhibited when attempting to build on that solid foundation. It was interesting that Paul never said anything negative about the people who followed him in leadership roles in the church. "Each builder must choose with care how to build on it," Paul wrote. The people within the church began making comparisons between Paul and Apollos. Some sided with Apollos, claiming that he was a better preacher, while others remained loyal to Paul. Such nonsense could not continue in the church. Paul simply laid the foundation in Jesus Christ, allowing others to come and build on what he began. Paul knew that divisive attitudes and behavior would harm the church.

The way we live our lives and how we conduct ourselves on a day-to-day basis says much of our faith. If people have trouble getting along with others in the church how can they ever hope to attract others into the fellowship? Unfortunately there are churches that have a reputation of fighting with each other or running their pastors out. When churches find themselves in that awkward position they fail to attract new people.

Paul wanted the people within that church to work together as a team. Each person possessed a different yet complementary gift that when used together would build up the church. We are incorporated into the body of Christ. Paul asks, "Do you not know that you are God's temple and that God's Spirit dwells in you?" The way we live should be markedly different from the rest of the world. Further, the church is more than brick and mortar; it is also people. We are the church together! We are God's temple with the Spirit dwelling in us.

A small rural church with an average worship attendance of only thirty people received a visitor one Sunday, a mother with a young child. It was evident that the child had special needs that required round-the-clock medical care. At first some of the members were put off by the depth of this family's need. Others found the situation disruptive to their worship experience.

Slowly church members were trained to help care for the child. The mother was grateful for the help and could run errands or get some much needed rest. The few children in the church would talk to the child and mother. The men helped alleviate accessibility issues in the family's home. The caring of the congregation completely changed the mother's life.

These acts of kindness also transformed the congregation. Worship attendance began to increase, the spirit of the congregation became more positive, and soon other families with young children began attending that church. Congregations that learn to treat others with the love of Christ attract people searching for a genuine sense of community.[1]

Living out our faith as part of the church makes us accountable to each other. When we see a sister or brother in the Lord acting in destructive ways we have a responsibility to confront the person "in Christian love." Paul was dead serious about this, "If anyone destroys God's temple, God will destroy that person." We must confront someone with the hope that the person will see the error of their ways and change their behavior. It is never easy but Jesus promises that in such situations he is present with us. In the context of a conflicted situation Jesus states, "For where two or three are gathered in my name, I am there among them" (Matthew 18:20).

Paul wanted the people to take a good, hard look at themselves and what they were doing. Were they encouraging one another in the faith or were they fighting with each other? Were they building one another up or tearing each other apart? According to Paul God does not take lightly destructive behavior within the church. People who cause damage will be answerable to God. "For God's temple is holy," Paul writes, "and you are that temple."

Elsewhere in his writing Paul asserts that believers need contact with other believers. We cannot be good Christians in isolation. We are called to live in community, to live a certain way, a holy way. We are to encourage one another in the faith. Being a part of the church of Jesus Christ entails responsibility. We are no longer free spirits who come and do as we please.

The bickering Corinthians thought they were wise, which Paul calls into question when he writes, "If you think that you are wise in this age, you should become fools so that you may become wise." We live out our faith not elevating ourselves, or making ourselves out to be better than other people, but rather as fools for Christ. Time and time again Paul modeled humility in how he related to the Corinthians.

Finally, all that we do, and all that we have belongs to God. Paul states, "All belong to you, and you belong to Christ, and Christ belongs to God." Everything we do we do for the glory of God as Paul claims later in his letter, "So, whether you eat or drink, or whatever you do, do everything for the glory of God" (1 Corinthians 10:31).

Richard Foster has written several popular books on prayer and spirituality. In one of them he recalled an experience he had as a teenager. He spent one summer with the Eskimo people in Alaska. "The Eskimo Christians I met there had a deep sense of the wholeness of life," he wrote, "with no break between their prayer and their work."

Richard had come with the attitude of adventure, of building the first high school above the Arctic Circle. However, it was hard work and far from the adventure he thought it would be. It was hard, backbreaking labor. One day he was digging a trench for a sewer line that he claimed was no small task in a world of frozen tundra. An Eskimo man whose face and hands displayed the leathery toughness of many winters watched him as he dug. "You are digging a ditch to the glory of God," he told the young man. Richard knew he said it to encourage him; he has never forgotten this man's words. "Beyond my Eskimo friend no human being ever knew or cared whether I dug that ditch well or poorly," Richard explained. "In time it was to be covered up and forgotten. But because of my friend's words, I dug with all my might, for every shovelful of dirt was a prayer to God.[2]

All of our activities, everything we do, needs to be evaluated using these terms. Paul teaches us, "For no one can lay any foundation other than the one that has been laid; that foundation is Jesus Christ." We order our personal lives and our corporate life in the church on the solid foundation of Jesus Christ. Amen.

---

1. Robert Schnase, *Five Practices of Fruitful Congregations* (Nashville: Abingdon, 2007), p. 93.
2. Richard J. Foster, *Prayer: Finding the Heart's True Home* (San Francisco: HarperSanFrancisco, 1992), p. 172.

Epiphany 8
Ordinary Time 8
1 Corinthians 4:1-5

Praise and Blame

"Where there is no vision, the people perish," the writer of the Old Testament book of Proverbs declares (Proverbs 29:18). Without a vision and an understanding of their mission, churches will continue to struggle and falter. Without a clear sense of identity people begin blaming each other over the plight of the church. People will blame their pastor or church leaders for the problems the church is experiencing. The church might even lose members; no one wants to be part of a church where members are in strong disagreement with each other over trivial matters.

"Where there is no vision, the people perish." Churches have been developing vision and mission statements for years. Some are precise and to the point, "to make disciples of Jesus Christ," or "to know Jesus and make him known," or "to live the Great Commission." Vision statements need to be short enough that people can remember and readily repeat them. When everyone in the congregation embraces their vision and mission, the church will continue its ministry in a positive direction. People will naturally be drawn to that church. People will proudly state what their church is doing in the community and around the world.

According to Bill Hybels "vision is a picture of the future that produces passion in you." A clear God-inspired vision will produce a passion in you — a passion that cannot be easily quenched.

A retired airplane pilot had fallen away from God during his high school days. The path he had chosen for himself led to destructive behavior. Later in life he surrendered his life to Christ. Today he is a leader in his church's high school and college group. For many years he has opened his home every Monday night to cook a meal for a group of students. He claims that Monday is his best day of the week.

A carpenter shares that while growing up his dad was never around to care for his family. His passion remains years later to offer free handyman assistance to a group of single mothers in the church.

A woman went through a gut-wrenching and humiliating divorce. During that time she had nowhere to turn. Today, she leads a divorce recovery ministry in her church.[1] "Vision is a picture of the future that produces passion in you." What are you passionate about?

The Corinthian congregation was in the midst of a conflict that if not soon resolved could destroy the church. The situation was serious. In that congregation some people who were critical of the apostle Paul while others were supportive of him. Some might even have blamed Paul for their present difficulties. In the midst of disagreements we should remember that Paul's goal was always to build up the church and never tear it down.

Paul experienced opposition firsthand. It seemed that everywhere he went he found himself in trouble. Whenever he spoke there were people who were offended or upset. Paul's devotion to Jesus Christ found him frequently arrested and in jail. Still, Paul had a clear understanding of his life mission; he was called and commissioned by Jesus himself. He passionately proclaimed the good news of Jesus Christ everywhere he went. With that strong sense of mission Paul traveled throughout the ancient world sharing the good news of Jesus and starting churches. Nothing would stop him. Not a ship wreck, not threats of physical harm, and not people who were critical of him! Nothing could curb Paul's passion.

Paul was not trying to win any popularity contest either. He did not depend on positive feedback from his listeners. Had he depended on accolades from others, his ministry might well have ended in frustration and despair early on. Paul kept his focus believing with all his heart that his reward was in heaven. The praise of others was not something that Paul sought. For Paul praise or blame really did not matter. Praise and blame was the same. He would continue to speak the gospel truth boldly despite the praise or blame he received.

This concept is something that we in the church need to embrace. We need to passionately go out sharing our faith in Jesus' name. We want others to discover for themselves the joy we have found in Jesus. There might be times when other people do not want to hear what we have to say, or have kind words for us, or maybe even call us names. We cannot allow such bad experiences to slow us down — we must continue. There may be times when we take a stand based on our faith that is viewed as unpopular among our peers. Paul teaches us that as long as we are speaking the truth it really does not matter what other people think of us, praise or blame is all the same.

In response to the problems the Corinthians were experiencing Paul wanted them to refocus on their vision and mission. Believers do not belong to themselves but are servants of Christ. Paul writes, "Think of us in this way, as servants of Christ and stewards of God's mysteries." The focus of ministry is not about ourselves and our perceived needs but rather about Jesus Christ. There are times, especially in the midst of congregational difficulties, when we need to be reminded that we are servants of the Lord. Servants are both trustworthy and accountable to their master.

We are servants of Jesus Christ. It may be difficult to view ourselves as servants. We live in a culture that values the movers and shakers, those who take charge and make a name for themselves. People do not always pay attention to servants; the term is frequently viewed in negative light. Unfortunately sometimes those attitudes creep into the church when people insist on their own way disregarding other people's feelings and ideas. People within the congregation who crave power and control always do more harm than good.

We should know our place; we are servants of Jesus Christ. Our agenda is to do the will of the master — Jesus. With everything we say or do we point not to ourselves but to Jesus. What God values is our faithfulness. "Moreover," Paul writes, "it is required of stewards that they be found trustworthy." Jesus trusts us to carry out the ministry that he began to the present and future. A question to ask ourselves is have we lived our lives in such a way that we are trustworthy?

Paul's message to the troubled Corinthians and to us today is instead of being critical and finding fault with each other we should spend that same energy as trustworthy servants in ministry. The servant has specific responsibilities and duties to perform. The servant will be held accountable.

David Sharp has been volunteering with inner-city, at risk teenagers for the last five years. When he first started David felt that this was what God wanted him to do, and he was filled with passion and enthusiasm. Those feelings wore off after the third or fourth week; he claims that he "was spinning my wheels." The teenagers were unruly, undisciplined, and out of control. "I found myself unsure if this was where I needed to be," he says of his experience, "but with prayer and soul searching, I kept showing up."

David continued volunteering at the center where over a period of several years he developed a special relationship with the teens. His attitude changed when he began viewing each teen as a precious gift from God. He continued to show them that he loved them and cared for them. As a result more young people began to come to the center.

One day as the teens were getting ready to board a bus to go home, there was an incident outside. David asked for help from a couple of the teens. After the situation was handled one of the teens told David, "We love you." Upon hearing those words David thought the teen was kidding, "Are you messing with me?" he asked. "No," the other said. "We love you; you really care about us."[2]

We strive to do our best and need not worry about what other people think of us. Only Jesus will judge us. Since ultimately the only person Paul would answer to was Jesus, he was not concerned with what other people thought of him. To Paul praise or blame really did not matter — to him it was all the same. Paul knew in his heart that he was a trustworthy servant. What people thought or did not think of him was of no concern to Paul. "But with me it is a very small thing that I should be judged by you or by any human court," Paul wrote, "I do not even judge myself."

Paul was quite confident in carrying out Jesus' ministry knowing that, "It is the Lord who judges me." We too can participate in outreach ministries with that same sense of confidence knowing that Jesus will judge each of us. Jesus "will bring to light the things now hidden in darkness and will disclose the purposes of the heart." Jesus will not be fooled by self-promotions. We may be able to fool others but we cannot fool Jesus. Instead of seeking status from each other, we need to recognize that it is the Lord who judges — that is the only commendation that matters.

The day will come when each one of us will stand in judgment. We on that day will be accountable to no one but God. We are not here to win popularity contests but to live out our faith in such a way as to glorify Jesus. Like Paul, praise or blame really does not matter to us, it is all the same. The business of praise and blame clearly belongs to God.

May our God-given vision propel us individually and as a church to carry out the ministry that Jesus began. And like Paul, may we stop at nothing. Amen.

1. Bill Hybels, *Holy Discontent* (Grand Rapids: Zondervan, 2007), p. 60.
2. David Sharp, "You Really Care," *Upper Room*, March 26, 2009, p. 33.

Epiphany 9
Ordinary Time 9
Romans 1:16-17; 3:22b-28 (29-31)

Everyone Is Invited

Every summer Kaitlin joins her youth group on mission trips. One summer the group traveled to New Orleans to help with the Hurricane Katrina relief. Their job was to clean out houses that had not been open since the hurricane. "As I entered the first untouched home," Kaitlin remembered, "the idea of caring and reaching to others really kicked in." Her first thought was to complain about the conditions but she said, "I knew if this were my own home that would be the last thing thought crossing my mind. I could not imagine the difficulty and the pain of walking into my own house after such destruction."

The experience of participating on mission trips has changed Kaitlin's life. "I continue to reach out to people within my community," she said. For Kaitlin helping other people provides an opportunity to share her faith, she explained, "I enjoy the warm feeling I get when I know I have impacted an individual by dribbling the slightest bit of faith into their heart."[1]

In a world with confused and competing loyalties Paul boldly claimed, "For I am not ashamed of the gospel." Paul was writing to the church of Rome, to people he had never met, to people who might have been unsure of their faith. It was dangerous to be a follower of Jesus Christ in a culture that claimed that the emperor was a god. Proclaiming the gospel of Jesus Christ was Paul's life mission and nothing or no one would prevent him from carrying out God's plan for his life. In making that bold claim Paul's life was in jeopardy but he unashamedly placed his life not in the hands of earthly rulers or authorities but in his Lord Jesus Christ.

Paul's goal in writing to the Romans was to bolster and strengthen their faith. The gospel, he wrote, "is the power of God for salvation to everyone who has faith." To experience "the power of God for salvation," all one has to do is believe in Jesus. It no longer mattered where someone was born because God's saving power was available to all people, in all classes, and circumstances of life. It was truly amazing to acknowledge that God had included all people in God's plan of salvation. The previous barriers were all knocked down, thanks to the life, death, and new life of Jesus Christ. It was now possible for all people to come to faith in Jesus Christ.

During Jesus' earthly ministry he worked first among those of Jewish descent, after his resurrection Jesus sent the disciples out into the entire the world. "Go therefore and make disciples of all nations," Jesus instructed his disciples, "baptizing them in the name of the Father and of the Son and of the Holy Spirit, and teaching them to obey everything that I have commanded you." Elsewhere in his writings the apostle Paul claimed, "There is no longer Jew or Greek, there is no longer slave or free, there is no longer male and female; for all of you are one in Christ Jesus" (Galatians 3:28).

The gospel message opened people's eyes to the possibility of faith in Jesus. The plan of salvation was God's intention from the beginning of time, but now it came to fruition. Those from a Jewish background were able to see how the promises they stood on had been fulfilled in Jesus. The Gentiles now understood that there was one true God. All the boundaries had been removed.

Further Paul writes, "The righteousness of God is revealed through faith for faith." God keeps God's promise made to the ancestors of faith in the Old Testament. Because God kept the covenant, all people receive faith in and through Jesus Christ. Faith in Jesus Christ yields salvation whereas the law always falls short. Through faith we are set into a right relationship with God. Paul makes his point by quoting the Old Testament prophet, Habakkuk, "The one who is righteous will live by faith." Faith means believing in Jesus, in all circumstances and not relying on one's lineage or the law. This is incredible good news, because it includes every one of us. The season of Epiphany serves to remind us of the importance of sharing the good news with all people in all places — Jesus is Lord of all.

"For there is no distinction," Paul writes as he continues to develop this important theme in the third chapter. In the kingdom of God no one has higher rank or standing because all those barriers have been broken down. Claiming that everyone stands on equal footing was a radical break with the present world of the Romans where there were different classes and social rankings. There is no distinction precisely because, "all have sinned and fall short of the glory of God." Sinful humanity cannot save itself but stands in need of God's grace.

What this means is that no person is exempt from being in a right relationship with God in and through Jesus Christ. We are "justified" made right through God's amazing grace. Grace is God's gift to us and is not something that we earn or even deserve; it is given to us freely from the God who loves each and every one of us. God's love for us is so strong that God stopped at nothing to restore our relationship. God's Son Jesus Christ suffered and died at the hands of a sinful humanity.

Jesus' death pointed to God's answer for sinful humanity and also God's sense of justice, truth, and faithfulness. Ultimately God has kept the covenant established with the heroes of faith. God sent Jesus to rescue us from the power of sin, something we cannot accomplish by ourselves.

To the Corinthians Paul wrote about the power of the cross. In times of confusion Paul advised believers to remember and look to the cross of Jesus. Elsewhere in his letter to the Romans Paul writes of the cross in terms of a sin offering. Again he draws from the Old Testament notion of the Day of Atonement. Paul declares that what God has done through Jesus Christ is once and for all — we are saved because of his sacrifice.

As we know the death of Jesus was not the end of the story — God raised Jesus to new life. "God put forward as a sacrifice of atonement by his blood, effective through faith." Through his death Jesus paid the price for all of our sins. Salvation is available to all people since as Paul stated God showed "no distinction" between people. This was God's plan from the beginning of time.

We live our lives by faith believing and trusting in Jesus. We cannot earn our salvation by following the letter of the law as some might have mistakenly thought. We are not saved by our good works either although Jesus demands much from us. We are saved only by God's grace! We can trust in Jesus knowing that he will never desert us. By trusting in Jesus we allow him to reshape our lives. The power of the gospel not only changes our lives but alters all of our relationships. The way we view ourselves and others is changed once we surrender everything to Jesus. Paul experienced that saving power in his own life. He was transformed from a fierce opponent of Christ to a zealous missionary.

Don Kimbro was going through a rough time in his life. "Everything I had worked so hard for was falling apart," he recalled, "my marriage, my family, and my business." Was this all he could expect from a lifetime of hard work — a life of sadness, disappointment, and failure, he reflected.

One day a local businessman stopped by his office to speak with him. Don immediately thought he was trying to sell him something. The gentleman promised that he would only take a few minutes of his time. He introduced himself as the owner of a local consulting firm. He explained that he was sharing with other business people in the community something that had changed his life as well as his business.

Don stated that he was short on time. The gentleman responded, "I want to talk to you about Jesus Christ and how knowing him can change your life." "You've got to be kidding," Don interrupted, "I'm in the biggest crisis of my life and you want to talk to me about religion?"

"I understand," the man replied. "I believe God can help." He reached into his pocket and handed Don a little booklet titled, "Steps to Peace with God." For the next few minutes he explained how much God loved him. He told Don what he needed was a new life. "God will totally redirect your life if you let him," he said. With that the man turned to leave, thanking Don for his time. Don sat there speechless. He tossed the booklet on his desk.

Six months later Don was cleaning out his office; his company was in the process of bankruptcy. As he was putting papers from his desk into a folder he found the booklet the visitor had left. He stopped what he was doing, sat down, and began reading. As he read he said he could almost hear the man's voice. He prayed the prayer on the back of the booklet, asking Jesus to forgive him and come into his life.

That was 25 years ago. Don said his life has never been the same. God dramatically changed his life. He never saw that gentleman who visited his office again, but Don says he expects to see him again in heaven.[2]

Could you be the person who shares Jesus with someone who is confused and hurting?

Faith and not works, grace and not law, and all humanity, not just some chosen few were the points Paul wanted the Romans to grasp. As we continue to live out our faith in Jesus Christ may we remember that we are saved in and through God's amazing grace and that grace includes all people. Everyone is invited; no one is excluded from God's grace. Amen.

1. www.thisibelieve.org.
2. Don Kimbro, "A Divine Appointment," *Today's Christian*, July/August 2005, Vol. 43, No. 4, 45.

The Transfiguration of Our Lord
(Last Sunday after Epiphany)
2 Peter 1:16-21

Credible Witnesses

Each one of us can remember those special transforming moments in our lives. We remember and can recall with great detail a life-changing experience. We describe such a time as once in a lifetime experience. Some of us might remember meeting an important person, or a celebrity, and gladly retell the story to anyone who will listen. We may recall a time when our faith came alive, when we met Jesus through the love of a Sunday school teacher, a friend, or a pastor. Those are the experiences we carry with us.

Carl has experienced the transforming power of God at work in his life. "From a young teenager," Carl claims, "I have seen and felt God in and through Jesus Christ mold and direct my life." Looking back over his sixty years Carl says that "God has truly been my strength in stressful and difficult times." His faith is more than just a Sunday habit, he claims, "God in my life has been a daily reality and defining force."

"God has helped me see through my own selfishness and pride to understand a bit, and truly only a bit," Carl reflects, "of the human condition."[1]

The disciples who traveled with Jesus must have also had those special memories of the events they witnessed firsthand during Jesus' earthly ministry. Later when they traveled from place to place teaching about Jesus they would recall their own personal experiences. The apostle Peter remembered well all the times he spent with Jesus. With great fondness he recalled the day when Jesus called him. At the time he was fishing and Jesus promised that from that moment he would be fishing for women and men for the kingdom of God. Peter willingly obeyed and began following Jesus. He did not know what the future would hold but he trusted Jesus. There were other events that Peter must have spoken about as he preached the gospel in an effort to convert new people to the faith. Some incidents probably made him smile, like the time he tried to walk on the water, became scared, and began to sink. Then Jesus' strong arms reached down to pull him to safety. Peter recalled with great detail his many experiences with Jesus even though decades had passed.

From time to time problems would arise among the believers and they would turn to the wise apostles for guidance. The book of Second Peter was concerned with false teachers who led the people astray presenting a serious problem. Peter tried his best to set the people on the right path once again. He clarified questions about the true identity and unique status of Jesus Christ.

With all the authority Jesus had given him, Peter tried to reassure the people, that what they were taught and believed was true. He wrote, "For we did not follow cleverly devised myths when we made known to you the power and coming of our Lord Jesus Christ, but we had been eyewitnesses of his majesty." Peter knew what he was talking about. He was present at all the critical moments in Jesus' earthly ministry. He was there when Jesus was led off to die on the cross, and he was present when the risen Lord appeared to the disciples. The life, death, and resurrection of Jesus Christ was not a fairy tale, a made-up story, or "cleverly devised myth" but was the truth. Peter was there as it happened. Now years later after growing in his faith and relationship with the Lord Jesus, Peter had a better understanding than ever.

First-century Christians had believed that the second coming of Jesus would certainly take place during their lifetimes. Decades had passed and still Jesus had not returned. When Jesus' triumphal return was delayed, the false teachers began telling the people that the whole notion was a "cleverly devised myth." Because Jesus had not returned they reasoned that it must not be true. The apostle Peter knew better and sought to set the matter straight once and for all. Peter knew how dangerous it would be to discard this foundational truth. The church would open itself to all sorts of irresponsible behavior.

Peter recalled the time when he accompanied Jesus along with fellow disciples, James and John to the mountain. While they were there a change came over Jesus. Then Jesus began speaking with two Old Testament prophets, Moses and Elijah. Like all such moments it was over too quickly. One minute Jesus was conversing with Moses and Elijah and the next he stood alone. As if that were not enough Peter and the other two disciples heard the voice of God speak, "This is my Son, my Beloved, with whom I am well pleased." Peter told the people, "We ourselves heard this voice come from heaven, while we were with him on the holy mountain." Today we refer to this event as the Transfiguration.

The Christian faith is real because of credible witnesses. Most of us are here today because someone loved us enough to share the story of Jesus with us. Then we claimed the faith for ourselves by accepting and believing in Jesus as our Lord and Savior. In turn we have a responsibility to share our faith with others, especially the next generation. Faith becomes real precisely because of other credible people. And so the Christian faith is passed from one generation to the next. Peter was older and knew that he would not live much longer; he wanted to make absolutely certain that the people had a proper understanding of the faith.

Not only was Peter an eyewitness to Jesus' life, death, and resurrection his certainty also stemmed from his understanding of the prophets. As he grew in his faith he came to understand that everything that happened to Jesus during his earthly ministry was in fulfillment of scripture. Prophets centuries before the birth of Jesus told of his coming. "So," Peter the wise elder stated, "we have the prophetic message more fully confirmed." Then he counseled his readers on the importance of paying attention to God's Word found in the scriptures. The Bible becomes for us, "a lamp shining in a dark place." We hold onto that Word as we would a light in the darkness for it provides direction, focus, and hope.

Peter wanted the people to understand that there was a difference between the prophets of old and the false teachers who were leading the people astray. Think for a moment of some of the Old Testament prophets. Some were reluctant to speak the word of the Lord. Some felt unworthy — remember Isaiah? "Woe is me!" he said, "I am lost, for I am a man of unclean lips." Other prophets were actually frightened. Who wants to tell people something they do not want to hear? Someone had to speak words of judgment to those who had the power to kill them. There could be dangerous consequences; some of the prophets even were stoned because of their convictions. It was a risky business to be a prophet. Apparently the false teachers did not share this sense of reluctant reverence as they misled the people.

The believers whom Peter was addressing did not have printed scriptures. They relied on prophets, preachers, and teachers to bring them the Word of God. The only reference they had was faithful individuals like Peter. We are fortunate today to have our own Bibles. The Bible has become "a lamp shining in a dark place." When people with questionable motives or teaching approach us we always have our Bibles to guide us. That is why it is important to read our Bibles so that we are not led astray. We are after all people of the book, the Bible. While we are strengthened by reading our Bibles daily, the scriptures truly come alive when we are with other believers, in Sunday school, Bible study, or worship. We come each week to hear God's Word for us. "No prophecy of scripture," Peter claimed, "is a matter of one's own interpretation." Peter was offering a word of caution to the believers. The false teachers who were causing problems were a little bit too sure of themselves or we might say loose in their interpretation of scripture. In the presence of other believers the Word of God comes alive.

The Bible is first and foremost about God and not us. Peter was clear about this "Because no prophecy ever came by human will, but men and women moved by the Holy Spirit." The prophecies of old were not devised by humans but by the power and prompting of the Holy Spirit.

We strive to be credible witnesses ourselves as we share the love of Jesus with others.

Roynell Young played professional football in the 1980s. "I retired from the game and we moved down to Houston," he said, "where I took a job selling insurance." As he drove through neighborhoods with aimless, hard-looking teenage boys clustered on corners, something kept nagging at him. "They reminded me of me," he said, "or what I would have been if there hadn't been a bunch of people looking out for me." He wondered who was looking out for them.

One day Roynell and a friend stopped and began playing basketball in one of those neighborhoods. When the youth first saw them they ran off thinking they were police officers. Three boys stayed to watch. After a few minutes Roynell challenged them to a game, "You beat us, I'll buy you all the pizzas and soda you can handle. We beat you; you sit down and talk with us."

Even though Roynell and his friend were older they won the pick up game and took the boys out for pizza anyway. He asked them about their family, neighborhood, and if they had considered their life's purpose. As they were leaving one of the youth asked if they would be back the next Saturday.

Before too long there were 100 youth; then 300! Roynell pooled some friends and they rented an old storefront across from the basketball court. The number of youth kept increasing, they soon ran out of space and had to move to a larger place, eventually they had enough money to open a charter middle school. Thinking of all the people who impacted his life, Roynell proudly claimed, "We're changing lives."[2]

Our faith is alive because of the faithful witness of others. We have the testimony of the apostles who were eyewitnesses to Jesus' teachings, miracles, and most importantly his life, death, and resurrection. We have the church where the scriptures are read and taught. And we have the Holy Spirit in our lives that prompts us to say and do things we could never say or do on our own. The Holy Spirit gives us the power we need to live out our lives as faithful modern day disciples of Jesus Christ. Amen.

---

1. www.thisibelieve.org.
2. Roynell Young, "Game Changer," *Guidepost*, March 2009, pp. 74-78.

www.ingramcontent.com/pod-product-compliance
Ingram Content Group UK Ltd.
Pitfield, Milton Keynes, MK11 3LW, UK
UKHW021303180426
11947UKWH00015B/994